I Can See Myself in His Eyeballs

Also by Chonda Pierce

Chonda Pierce on Her Soapbox
It's Always Darkest Before the Fun Comes Up

God is closer than you think

I Can See Myself in His Eyeballs

Chonda Pierce

ZondervanPublishingHouse

Grand Rapids, Michigan

A Division of HarperCollinsPublishers

I Can See Myself in His Eyeballs
Copyright © 2001 by Chonda Pierce
Requests for information should be addressed to:

▟ZondervanPublishingHouse

Grand Rapids, Michigan 49530

ISBN 0-7394-1800-9

Published in association with the literary agency of Wolgemuth & Associates, Inc.

Interior design by Melissa Elenbaas

Printed in the United States of America

To World Outreach Church

in Murfreesboro, Tennessee, and to my pastors,

Allen Jackson and Phillip Jackson,

who are constantly pointing out to me

the never-ending handiwork

of a loving and merciful God in a very chaotic world

(starting with their wives—Kathy and Angela)

Contents

Prologue: Eyeball to Eyeball   9

1. Momma Takes New York   13

2. A Day at the Beach   21

3. If God Had Meant for You to Have
Holes in Your Ears . . .   27

4. The Tower of Terror   31

5. *¡Yo Quiero, Jesus!*   37

6. Momma's Big Knife   43

7. A Close Blush with the Law   49

8. Manhattan Takes Us   55

9. The Great Diaper Derby   65

10. The Dog That Ate My Living Room   73

11. Our Family Reunion in a Minivan   81

12. Showtime at the Nursery   89

13. Still Trying to Get It through My Thick Head   95

14. Footloose and Fancy Free   101

15. I Once Owned a Chevette   105

16. You'll Never Have to Dust Again   111

17. Truck-Stop Rose   119

18. Papaw's Shiny Red Truck   123

19. Salvation in the Driveway   129

20. Twins?!   135

21. Noisy Mimes in Indianapolis   141

22. Dancing in the Living Room   147

23. You Can't Grow Macaroni   153

24. The Septic Tank Man   161

25. I Think I Just Locked My Keys in the Car   167

26. All the Ice Cream You Can Eat   173

27. The Christmas Surprise Surprise   181

28. The Holy Ghost in New Orleans   185

29. The Blue Knight Picks My Daughter   191

Epilogue: Face to Face   199

Eyeball to Eyeball

My son, Zachary, and I scheduled a mother-son night while my husband and daughter were off climbing a mountain somewhere in the western half of the United States. Zach and I rented some movies, popped some popcorn, fluffed the pillows, and settled in to fight fat grams and sleep.

At the end of our second movie, I looked over at Zach and was surprised to find him still awake. All I could see in the dim light from the television was his tiny face; the rest of him was snuggled under the covers.

"Hey, Mom," he said, "let's tell stories."

I turned over on my side so I could see him better. "Okay, Zach. What kind of stories? And don't say 'ghost stories' either."

For a long time he didn't say anything. I thought maybe he was thinking about it. But after he had had enough time to think, he still hadn't said anything. He kept staring at me. Then, slowly, he pushed aside the pillows and blankets and moved so close that our noses were almost touching. Right into my eyes he continued to stare.

I couldn't stand it any longer. "Zach, what *are* you doing?"

As if he were afraid any noise would spook away whatever it was he had spotted, he whispered, "Mom, I can see myself in your eyeballs."

For the next several days I wondered what it would be like to see ourselves in God's eyes, to see our images reflected because we were so close to him. *Close to him*. I don't want to see myself in God's eyes just because I want to see myself. (That's what the little mirror over the car's sun visor is for.) What I really want is to get close to God so I can know him better.

That night I learned from Zachary that to see God I have to spot him, and then I have to keep moving closer to him, like Zach crawling over the pillows that night to get a good look at me.

Okay, so maybe it's easier to spot God, to recognize his presence, when something good happens, like at a baby christening or a revival or a wedding. But can I see God in the hard times? The ugly times? Like when I get a speeding ticket, when my daughter wrecks her grandfather's truck, when a plane crashes, or when a big chunk of St. Patrick's Cathedral falls on my head. Where is God in all that?

Not long ago I read a devotional by Charles Henry Parkhurst, a nineteenth-century minister who wrote about young David slaying a lion long before he ever fought Goliath. The lion, Parkhurst said, was "God's opportunity in disguise." Had David not succeeded there, he might never have faced Goliath (probably because he would have been that lion's lunch). Then I read, "May the Lord open our eyes to see him, even in temptations, trials, dangers, and misfortunes."

So God makes himself known when we are in an angry lion's presence. But—and here's the catch I'm trying to work through in these pages—we have to open our eyes.

This past year I've tried to keep my eyes from slamming shut. I've peered intently around me so I'll see God's presence in some of the most unlikely places—like the day my husband stabbed himself with the knife Momma had hidden in her purse, or when a clunky, sweaty knight in armor honored my daughter by making her princess of the castle, or the time I drove a Chevette held together by wire clothes hangers.

I'm still gazing and squinting. And, as Zachary did that night on the pillow, I'm inching closer and closer to God. I see him when my husband takes me dancing in our living room; I see him when the dog eats the sofa; I see him when the vacuum cleaner salesman shows up at the door. I want to see God in all these moments because I want to be close to him "when the lion comes"—close enough so I can see myself in his eyeballs.

Momma Takes New York

For since the creation of the world God's invisible qualities — his eternal power and divine nature — have been clearly seen, being understood from what has been made, so that men are without excuse.

ROMANS 1:20

Sometimes when I'm traveling to a place I know my momma would love to see, like New York, I take her along. Some of you may know Momma. She's been in my videos, and she's traveled with me on the road. But for those of you who don't know her, she's about five feet tall, born and raised in central Kentucky, graduated from Oddville High School, and traveled as far as Myrtle Beach, South Carolina. Not until she hooked up to cable TV in the late '80s did she catch a glimpse of other parts of the world. So when the opportunity came to travel to New York with me, she rushed right out to Wal-Mart and bought one of those suitcases with a pullout handle and rollers so she wouldn't "slow us down."

Momma finds such joy in simple things—like the woman working the little market in the airport. Mom said she was going for some gum, so I sat at the gate and waited . . . and waited . . . and waited. Finally I grabbed our carry-on luggage and went to find her. She was in the little market chewing gum and chatting with the cashier. I signaled for her to come over to me, and she made a few small steps my way, but not before waving to her new friend and saying, "I'll be praying for your niece, now."

"What was that all about?" I asked.

"Oh, you mean Margaret?" She pointed to the little woman behind the gum counter. "She's the nicest young lady. She told me all about her sister and her husband, who just got laid off from his computer programming job, but he's really, really good and hopes he has another job lined up this weekend. Her sister's doing okay, too, cleaning houses and working part-time at the grocery store. But their daughter, her niece, wants to get a tattoo. Oh, my." Mother just shook her head. "You help me pray for that family too, Chonda." I nodded and tugged Mom toward the gate.

We had to change planes in Newark, New Jersey, another place Mother had never been. "I can't believe I'm here in Newark," she sang. "Any famous people from Newark? I wonder what sort of restaurants they have in Newark. Now what state is Newark in?"

"We're in New Jersey, Mom," I said. "Just across the river from New York City."

Her eyes lit up.

"I'm going to buy a cup of coffee, Mom," I said. "While I'm gone, you can look out that window over there," and I pointed. "I think you can see the New York City skyline."

I must have been gone a good fifteen minutes because I couldn't find the French vanilla cream I wanted for my coffee. When I returned to the window, Mom was still there, pressed up against the glass. "Mom, can you see the city?"

Mom turned around slowly, tears streaming down her face. She dabbed at her eyes with her coat sleeve and sniffled as if she had a bad cold. "I can't believe this."

I knew I should have just gone with the regular cream. I shouldn't have left her for so long.

"What is it, Mother?"

"I just saw the Statue of Liberty," she said through tears. "I never thought I would live to see the Statue of Liberty. Oh, honey, thank you for bringing me along. God is so good to me, so faithful. This is the best day of my life!"

I gave her a napkin, draped my arm across her shoulders, and led her away from the glass. "Here, have some coffee."

She pushed away the cup. "No thanks, honey. I don't care for French vanilla."

I did a concert that night in Buffalo, New York, and introduced everyone to my mother. I even brought her up on the stage and gave her the microphone so she could say hello.

"I just love this state," she started. "You have so much to be proud of. Buffalo is the most gorgeous city I have ever seen. I never thought I would ever be here, in New York. This is a dream come true. This is really a gorgeous city. But, oh my, it's so cold here. It worries me a little bit because y'all might not think hell looks so bad when it's this cold, but I

Momma Takes New York

am glad Chonda brought me here. This is the best night of my life. I'll never ever forget—" I grabbed the microphone. But the audience loved my mother and gave her a standing ovation.

The next day, I was scheduled to drive over to Toronto to tape a television show, which I thought would be too grueling for Mom. But when I stepped out of the shower bright and early the next morning, she was up.

"Mom, why don't you sleep in?" I said. "Take it easy."

"Are you kidding?" she said. "Bonnie and Carol are meeting me in the lobby in a half hour to take me to Niagara Falls."

"Bonnie and Carol? But Mom, it's cold, and you have to get in and out of the car, and you were up late last night and—"

"It's Niagara Falls!" she said, almost scolding me. "You think I'm going to come this close to Niagara Falls and miss it?" She cinched up her coat and asked me to help her with the hood.

"Just don't get too close to the edge," I cautioned, pulling her furry hood down close to her eyes. For just a moment I thought about when I was a kid at my grandmother's house in Kentucky and Mom would bundle me up in fourteen layers of clothes so I wouldn't freeze when I went out sledding.

When I returned that night, I could tell Mom was back and already had eaten a good meal because of all the dishes stacked outside her door. She greeted my knock with, "Oh, honey, I'm so glad you're back. This is the greatest hotel. You push that little button on the telephone—the one with the picture of the knife and fork—and they bring you whatever you want to eat. And besides that, that little refrigerator over there is full of snacks—peanuts, chips, cold drinks. I think the church must have put them there. And downstairs is a beauty shop that fixed my hair better than I believe it's ever been fixed. And they won't take any money, either."

"No?"

"Oh no, honey. They just ask for my room number. Isn't that nice?"

I nodded and smiled, hoping she could see that her happiness made me happy too. "How was Niagara Falls?"

Her countenance seemed to melt as she recalled the scene. She put away her chips and brushed the salt from her hands, but before she could speak she began to cry. "It was the most beautiful thing I've ever seen."

"More beautiful than the Statue of Liberty?"

"I never thought I would live to see Niagara Falls."

"Well, what did it look like?"

She tried to tell me. She started with the color, then tried to capture the sound, then tried to capture the magnitude, but she never got too far before she would throw her hands in the air in futility. She dabbed at her tears with her hand. I found a napkin left over from room service and gave it to her. She wiped her nose and said, "This was the best day of my life. And I got pictures, lots of pictures."

A few days later, back home again, Mom came over, carrying a stack of glossy photos she had taken in New York. A few were of me on stage with a microphone in my hand. They could have been taken anywhere. But then I came to the ones she had been excited about, the ones of Niagara Falls.

She had bought one of those cheap, disposable cameras from the gift shop at the falls and had someone snap a shot of her standing in front of the falling water. Lots of snow was on the ground, so the whole photo was framed in the whitest of white. Water, the color of diamonds beneath a lamp, sparkled as it stood frozen in the photo, like the ice that covered the river's rocky edges. The scene reminded me of the old Frosty the Snowman cartoon in which every tree, lamppost, and park bench is covered with a thick frosting.

And then there was Mother. Picture after picture showed Mom with her new friends Bonnie and Carol by the falls (Mom appeared way too close to the edge, but that could have been a deceiving angle), in the snow, by the gift shop. In each photo Mom's fuzzy hood framed her face, her nose as red as Rudolph's was.

I soaked up the pictures, checked the backs of them to make sure they weren't postcards Mom had purchased in the gift shop. They were incredible, and I was sorry I had missed the sight.

But Mom had seen it. Mom, who wasn't going to miss it for anything.

"They're good, aren't they?" she said about the pictures. I was afraid she would start to cry again, so I offered her a cup of coffee and told her I was packing to leave the next day.

"Where are you going?" she asked, tucking her pictures into her purse.

"California," I told her.

Her eyes lit up. "California? Oh, I've always wanted to see California. Do you know they have trees bigger around than this house? And mountains, and the Golden Gate Bridge, and ... and my suitcase is still packed! Oh, this will be wonderful, honey. This will be the best day of my life!"

Momma walks around with her eyes wide open because she doesn't want to miss a thing God is doing. When he paints a picture, she wants to make sure she sees every brush stroke. And when the curtains on the window are pulled back, she wants to press right up against the glass and thank God for the view, which is a very good thing since I didn't have the heart to tell her that what she thought was the Statue of Liberty was really a barge with a crane on it unloading some steel.

A Day at the Beach

Be merciful, just as your Father is merciful.

LUKE 6:36

There's nothing like a late-night telephone call from the local police department to shake up your day.

My best friend, Alison, owns a place near Charleston, South Carolina, just off the coast. For the last several years I have gone there for at least a week to do nothing but eat, sleep, shop, and shop. For me, it's a place to park my brain and to replace all the city air in my lungs with ocean air.

But this particular year, late at night, while Alison and I were in a heated battle of Rummikub (only the greatest board game ever invented), the phone rang. Alison's son, Justin, answered. After a short moment all the blood drained from his face, and we heard him say, "You'd better talk to my momma." Alison took the phone and held it so we both could hear.

"Sorry to bother you so late tonight, ma'am," the nasal voice said. "My name is Sergeant Lipton, and I'm just making a few routine calls to residents of the community to say we believe we're close to an arrest of Crazy Eddie."

"Crazy Eddie?"

"Yes, ma'am. If you've been listening to the news, you're probably aware of his escape earlier in the day. We've been all over this island with dogs and cops and soldiers and swamp buggies. And now—"

"So he's still loose?" Alison interrupted. Her husband was working two hundred miles away, and David wasn't supposed to fly in until the next day. So there we were in a tiny beach house, Alison and me, with three children and a crazy man who had just escaped from prison and had somehow outrun a swamp buggy.

"Well . . . he's sort of loose," said Sergeant Lipton.

"Sort of loose? How can he be sort of loose?" said Alison.

"Because it's late, and he's probably exhausted after wrestling the gators and—"

"What are you talking about?"

"Well, we had him cornered in a swamp on the island's southeast side, and a gator jumped him and . . ."

"And what?"

"And he killed the gator and got away."

"He what?!"

"But like I said, we're really close to an arrest."

"How can you be so sure?" I called into the receiver.

"Because we've cornered him at the Seaside Mall," Sergeant Lipton continued and then paused as Alison and I wondered what that had to do with anything. "And if I've done my homework right, ma'am," he added, "one good mall—no matter what part of the country it's in—can literally suck the life out of any man, no matter how strong or how crazy he might be."

Something clicked inside my head, and I took the receiver from Alison, who had also turned very pale by now. "David, is that you?" I asked.

Sergeant Lipton–Crazy Eddie–David began to cackle on the other end.

"That's not funny," I told him. "It's David," I said to Alison, and the blood began to return to her face, faster than was probably healthy.

"I'm going to kill him," she said, not caring how many witnesses overheard.

"Just settle down, Alison," I told her after I'd finished "speaking" with David and hung up the phone. "Besides, he won't be here until tomorrow."

David came in late the next day and couldn't wait to go down to the beach. Alison and I had cooled down a bit, but we still made David carry the cooler, the towels, and all the beach toys for the two-blocks walk.

"I can't believe you guys fell for that," said David, as he tottered barefoot down the drive, arms full of beach stuff. Alison and I didn't say a word, trying not to encourage him. "I mean, Sergeant Lipton! I made up the name from a tea box right there on the spot. Hahahahahahahahaha!"

I heard Alison say, just before we reached the end of the drive, "You know, you might want to wear some sandals. It's been very hot, and the road might be—"

A Day at the Beach

"Ouch! Ouch!" David whooped as he danced around in a tiny circle. The cooler lid flopped open and closed, all the beach towels slid to the ground, plastic shovels and buckets flew off to the right and left. "Hot! Hot! Hot!" he yelled. On his tiptoes, trying to find a way off the hot pavement, he made a beeline for the skinny grassy island in the median.

Again I heard Alison say, just before he got there, "Watch out for the sandspurs!"

But David had already hopped onto the sandy, grassy patch and, for just a second, seemed to find relief. His peaceful expression didn't last long, though, before his face twisted into the most painful expression I'd ever seen. He raised one foot and lowered it and then raised the other, as if he were climbing invisible stairs. Whenever he would lift a foot we could see all sorts of sticks and grass and prickly things stuck to the bottom—stuff he couldn't shake off.

Sandspurs!

I'm not sure who started to laugh first. It may have been me, or Alison, or perhaps even the children. All I know is that we were laughing so hard we could barely stand up. I couldn't catch my breath. Tears began to flow down Alison's face. The children were hopping around like David and cackling and laughing. Alison managed to pull her video camera from its bag and start to shoot, but the video is so bouncy it's hard to watch.

David lay on his back on the hot pavement and stuck both feet straight up in the air. The bottoms of them were covered with the prickly, green sandspurs.

"Oh, my feet! Oh, my back! Oh, my feet! Oh, my back!" David wailed on and on so that we could hardly hear ourselves laughing. When he tried to sit up to get his back off the hot pavement, his feet would touch the ground, and he would scream and then roll onto his back and scream some more.

Alison finally came to the rescue and made him roll over onto one of the big beach towels. (This is where the video begins to steady somewhat, and we can get a better look at all the sandspurs in the bottoms of his feet.)

"Oh, my," you can hear Alison say on the video. I'm still cackling. Zach is pointing and laughing, and Chera and Justin are falling all over each other, red faced and near tears.

That day convinced me that God is still working on me (and Alison) because—after a bit—both of us began to pick off the little prickly things from the bottoms of David's feet and toss the stickers to the side. David just lay there in the middle of the drive, legs raised high and feet swaying back and forth in the breeze that blew in from the ocean (which we never made it to that day) repeating, "Ouch, that hurts. Ouch, that hurts."

"Okay, Sergeant Lipton," Alison said. "This will probably hurt a little—but not as much as wrestling gators."

Pluck. Pluck.

"Ouch, that hurts. Ouch, that hurts."

After several long minutes, we helped David hobble back to the house. We split up the towels and toys between the kids, and Alison and I carried the cooler back home.

Weeks later I finally sorted through what had happened. (Before that, every time I'd get close, I'd start to laugh, and that's as far as I could get.) Eventually I could see God's mercy playing out that day. I realized that no matter how much we'd like to see someone get what's coming to him, there's always a place for compassion, for mercy. No matter how much David had frightened us the night before, it was right for us to help him when he needed us.

Now, I think Alison still has some sorting out to do. When I asked her what she learned from that experience, she simply said, "That God can use even a lowly sandspur to dole out justice upon his people when they stray."

Give it time. I believe she's still a bit upset with Sergeant Lipton.

If God Had Meant for You to Have Holes in Your Ears . . .

May your whole spirit, soul and body be kept
blameless at the coming of our Lord Jesus Christ.

1 THESSALONIANS 5:23B

I sat pinched and tense on a padded stool in a jewelry story in the mall. In the mirror I watched the woman standing behind me. She held a small, shiny gun pointed to the ceiling, and she grinned. "You might feel a little sting." She grabbed hold of one of my earlobes and brought her gun down to meet it. I closed my eyes, and my momma's words rang loud in my ears: "If the Lord had meant for you to have holes in your ears, he would have put them there!"

I grew up with two sisters, and we heard that a lot. But I was eighteen and in college now; I had moved out of our house and into the dorm. So I had marched into the jewelry store with an air of defiance, and I had told the woman behind the counter, "Pierce my ears. I am a woman . . . *and my momma's not here.*"

All it took was two quick shots. Ouch! Ouch! I had holes in both earlobes.

When I walked out the door, I had taken only a couple of steps, with the tiny starter set shining in my sore earlobes, when two nuns dressed in black and white walked by. I just knew it was a sign from God! I took those earrings out right there and never put them in again.

Until I work up the nerve to try again, clip-ons work fine for me. Besides, should Gabriel blow his trumpet while I'm sporting a pair of earbobs, I can slip those things right off and I'll be ready to go! Some of these young people today are going to have a hard time. They had better hope it's a *long* song—long enough to pull out everything from their ears, noses, cheeks, tongues, and belly buttons!

To tell you the truth, I used to think God showed himself in the form of nuns walking through a mall, or preachers pacing back and forth on television, or in shadows on the side of a refrigerator that showed up only between 4 and 5 P.M.—and could be seen only if you happened to be hanging upside down in a certain tree in the front yard. I thought God showed up only in miraculous ways, in ways out of the ordinary, in ways that seemed foolish. That's how we would know it was him, like some sort of a secret Christian code. And if you didn't know the code, then you must not be a Christian.

I was wrong. And I'm so glad that's not how it works.

I wish I had talked to the two nuns that day. I wish I had bought them a big sandwich at the food court. Something tells me if I had, they might have even blessed my new ears, might have even said something like, "God loves your ears—in any old condition. What he's *really* concerned with is the condition of your heart. Now, pass the salt."

The Tower of Terror

For where your treasure is, there your heart will be also.

LUKE 12:34

You leave a grown man and his two kids by themselves for one day in Florida and what do they do? They fall from a ten-story building and just laugh about it.

We had been in Orlando for a couple of days, playing at Disney World. Then I had to go to some interviews at the Christian Booksellers Association convention—boring stuff for kids and a dad to attend. So I told them to go on along without me. Go to the MGM Theme Park and experience some rides, see some shows, eat some junk food, and have a blast while I sit in stuffy, crowded rooms and listen to speeches. Don't feel sorry for me. Just go!

So they did. I figured I must have taken the wrong approach.

That evening we all met up at the hotel. That's when I heard about the Tower of Terror.

"Oh, Mom, it was great," Zach, our nine-year-old son, told me while I wiped crusted cotton candy from his chin. "We rode up into the Tower of Terror—"

"Tower of Terror?" I said.

"Yeah, this old haunted hotel that's ten stories high, and when you get to the top, the car falls through this hole and—"

"Fell? Ten stories? Are you all right?" I checked the top of his head for bumps.

"Mom," Zach said, shaking free, "it was just a ride. We were all strapped in." Then he paused as he cut a glance over at his father (who also had some dried cotton candy on his chin) and said, almost slyly, "But Dad got pretty scared."

David gave his best I-don't-know-what-you're-talking-about expression and said, "I don't know what you're talking about."

Chera, who was fifteen at the time, grinned and said, "No one else in the car was curled up in a fetal position and crying."

"I wasn't crying," David protested. "The wind was blowing in my eyes and making them water. Now tell your mother the rest of the story."

"I don't know what fetal position means," Zach said, "but when we got to the end of the ride, there were some pictures of us on this big board, and Dad was all curled up in a ball in the corner of the car. How embarrassing!"

"Tell your mother the *rest of the story*," David said again.

"Oh, about how you sat on the ice cream cone and—"

"No, no, the rest of the *other* story—about the Tower of Terror."

"Why don't you tell it, Dad?" Chera said. "Since you were the one who was so scared."

"*I wasn't scared*," David countered. "But I'll tell it anyway."

David adjusted his wrinkled shirt and began. "Okay, so we went up into the Tower of Terror, ten stories high. And people all along the way were wearing these fake bellhop and butler uniforms, and there were cobwebs, dust, and scary music, and some people were screaming and crying, but I was just glad to be going on a fun ride with my two children."

Chera and Zach rolled their eyes, but David continued. "Now, it would have been helpful had there been some orientation session beforehand, you know, to kind of prepare you for what was going to happen once you reached the top."

"You fall, Dad," Chera offered her brief orientation. "What part of 'fall' didn't you understand?"

"I knew we were going to fall," David said. "I just didn't know it would be so soon. I mean, we'd just reached the tenth floor. We had passed a couple of shaking doors and heard some rattling chains, but I figured we'd tour around a bit more. See some sights, maybe even count down from ten. You know, to give us a chance to hang on or something."

"Or curl up," Zach said with a big grin.

"I wasn't *that* curled up."

"Yes you were," Zach insisted. "Tell her about the picture."

"First, let me tell her about the fall," he said, "then she will appreciate the picture even more." David looked up at

The Tower of Terror

me, and as his face seemed to wilt, he said, "The fall was horrible." His lip trembled, and I moved to hold him, but he stopped me with an upraised hand. "Let me finish," he said. "With no warning at all, the bottom just dropped out, and my life flashed before my eyes. I could see you and the kids and the vacation we took to Myrtle Beach when Chera was five and the pets back home and that old car—that Chevette we had that kept bursting radiator hoses—remember that? And it was so dark in there, and the kids were screaming—"

"Happy screams," Chera interjected, and Zach nodded.

"Anyway, before I could gather my senses, the ride was over, and a skinny kid in a butler suit was telling us all to please exit the car."

"We had to pull Dad up from the corner," Zach said with a giggle.

"I thought I'd dropped something," David said. "I was just making sure."

"In the picture your eyes were closed," Chera said.

"Yeah, yeah, the picture." David's tone seemed to suggest he couldn't argue with that. "And the picture is exactly why we went back."

"You went back?"

"Yeah!" Zach almost screamed. "And you should have seen Dad *that* time."

David smiled real big. "Yup, we went back. And at nighttime, when all the screams and shadows and cobwebs were even scarier." David took a deep breath and pushed out his chest. "Only this time when the kids threw up their arms, I threw up my arms; when they screamed, I screamed. My stomach went up into my head and tried to come out my ears. Air went up my nose and came out my mouth. My ears popped, and my neck snapped, and I had a half-dozen near-death experiences. But I kept my arms up and wide open."

"That's the way you're *supposed* to ride it, Dad," Chera said.

"In the picture," Zach said, "Dad was just like this." And Zach threw up his arms, his head back, his mouth open, and his eyes bugged out. "He looked awesome!"

"Did you buy a picture?" I had to see this.

David, Chera, and Zach exchanged looks. Zach said, "Yeah, Dad, where's the picture?"

David looked back at me and said, "We didn't exactly get one. Not one you can hold anyway." Then his face brightened as he said, "But there is one in here," and he pointed to Zach's head. "And in there," and he pointed to Chera's head. "*That's* where the pictures are."

Now it was in my head too. I could see him, hair flying up, lips peeled back over his teeth, arms like noodles in the wind, his two children beside him, like little clones, sharing the same ride and the same laughs.

David knew, as I do, that the best pictures are those you save in your head, the ones put there by those you love and those who love you. God has filled my head with pictures again and again and again, pictures far more valuable than any material gift could be: landscapes, faces, expressions, smells, tastes, and touches. Pictures of a father and son who rip off their shirts and wrestle on the living room floor until someone gets a bad carpet burn or until they tip over the little table by the front door with the vase on it. Pictures of father and daughter with backpacks strapped on and heading out the front door to climb a mountain, looking like a pair of armadillos.

This is how God shows his love to me: through the actions of a father who loves his children—even if that means screaming like a madman and throwing up his arms into the air on the Tower of Terror, *twice*.

¡Yo Quiero, Jesus!

As soon as Jesus was baptized, he went up out of the water. At that moment heaven was opened, and he saw the Spirit of God descending like a dove and lighting on him.

MATTHEW 3:16

The first time I ever saw her I wanted to jump onto a chair and scream. She had a tiny body; a long, sleek tail; a little head with big, fanlike ears; and giant brown eyes. She was white as a snowball except for some brownish smudge marks on her back.

"Mommy," Zach said, holding the ratlike animal in the cradle of his arms. I noted the creature was wrapped in one of my good towels. "This is Frisket—because she's so frisky—my new Chihuahua!" (And I used to fuss at him for getting too much hot sauce at Taco Bell.)

I already had agreed to let this . . . this "item" into my house, and now it was looking at me and twitching its nose as if *I* didn't smell so good.

I don't know why I had said yes. Maybe it was Zach's pleading voice. You know the voice, "Please, please, please, Mommy. Can I? Can I? I'll clean my room every day for the rest of my life!" Maybe that was it.

Or maybe it was Zach's nine-year-old eyes—eyes that sparkled and came close to watering up and spilling out tears. Or maybe it was the way he had disappeared into his room and then returned a few minutes later with quarters, dimes, nickels, and pennies (lots of pennies), piled them up on the kitchen counter, and said it was all he had. Now could he *please* buy the puppy?

It must have been one of those reasons because I never would have said yes to a dog in my house—a Chihuahua, which I'm still not totally convinced is a member of the dog family.

But I had said yes, and Zach had checked the newspapers. Every day he would pore over the classifieds, looking for someone who had a Chihuahua for sale. He found one in a town nearby, and he and his father drove—under cover of dark—to the parking lot of a restaurant and met the dog's owner. They gave her the money, and she gave them the dog. It seemed like the proper way to buy a Chihuahua to me, especially after I saw her that first time in the brightness of the kitchen.

After a few days I saw how Zach loved that dog. He fed and watered her way too much, so that there was a mess not only around the dish but also throughout the house.

At times I couldn't stand her. I'd catch a glimpse of her darting behind the chair or couch—just a glimpse—and I'd

squeal and tap dance around the living room floor, screaming, "Mouse! Mouse!"

I'll admit, though, that she had her cute moments. Like
the times when she would try to leap up onto the couch but
couldn't quite make it and would plop flat on her back. (Was
I wrong to laugh at that?)

And I thought it was pretty funny when a Taco Bell commercial would come on and Zach would hold up Frisket to
the TV until she was face-to-face with her cousin, who was
advertising a chalupa. "Oh, look at that, Frisket," Zach would
say. "Look at your cousin on TV. Don't you want a chalupa,
Frisket?" Of course she would never answer and never
seemed to want a chalupa either. So Zach would set her on
the floor, and I'd call her over to the couch and watch her
jump, smash into the couch (thud!), bounce off, and land on
her back (plop!). During those times, she was really cute.

At bedtime I'd toss—I mean, lift—Frisket from the floor so
she could curl up on the pillow next to Zach, where she would
lay all night until I'd toss—I mean, lead—her to the backyard.

Because Zach loved his Chihuahua so much, people gave
him stuffed Chihuahuas, with which he covered his bed. One
day someone gave him an oversized T-shirt with a big Chihuahua face on the front.

Zach held Frisket up to his shirt one day and said, "See?
See your cousin? Look at that Chihuahua on my shirt." He
stretched the material with one hand and poked Frisket's face
into his shirt with his other. But Frisket didn't seem to care
about the picture on Zach's shirt so I called her to the couch.
(Thud! Plop!)

Maybe it was the fact that something so tiny could make
messes that were so giant. Maybe it was the way she would

sidle right up to anyone (company included) and flip over onto her back and beg to have her pink, hairless belly rubbed. Maybe it was the way her hipbones poked out like old chicken bones in a handkerchief. Whatever it was, just looking at that dog made me wince, made me want to jump up on the table so she couldn't get to me, made me want to slap the edge of the couch and say, "Here, girl! Jump up here (if you can)!" At least that's how I felt about Frisket until Zach got baptized.

Months before he got Frisket, Zach had asked Jesus to live in his heart. He was lying on the living room floor, watching a Jesus movie, when suddenly he squeezed his eyes shut and his lips started flying with words no one could hear.

"What are you doing, Zachary?" I asked.

His lips stopped, and he cracked open one eye and whispered, "I'm asking Jesus into my heart."

I let him carry on and prayed right along with him, my eyes squeezed just as tight as his. Later, while I tucked him in, we talked about what his prayer had meant, and Zach seemed happy to let Jesus live there in his heart.

I walked into our room where David was reading and announced, "By George, I think he's got it."

David grinned and said, "My name's David. But praise the Lord anyway."

At church we have a big baptism once a month. The congregation gathers by the baptistery so the first thing the one being baptized hears on his or her way up from the water is "Glory to God!" along with some shouting and hand-clapping—a real saintly celebration. We checked the calendar for the next scheduled baptism, and Zach said he was ready.

A few minutes before church started, we went to a short question-and-answer class led by our pastor, ate pizza, and laughed about what bribe would convince the pastor to hold someone under longer than others.

Since our church doesn't do the all-white robe for baptizing, each candidate is asked to bring along some old knock-around clothes that don't matter if they get wet. Zach wore some old swim trunks and a T-shirt—the one with the big, mousy-looking Chihuahua on the front. Above the picture of the little animal was the phrase *¡Yo quiero, Jesus!* At the time we picked out the knock-around clothes, I thought the shirt would be cute, but the writing was so small all anyone could really see was the big dog head, eyes bulging, ears stuck out like funeral fans, and high cheekbones.

I watched Zach, my son, walk slowly down the steps, test the water with his toes, and then step down so the Chihuahua on his shirt slowly went under the water. Part of me was overwhelmed with joy to see my child enter the water just as Jesus had done so many generations before, to be immersed in the waters that signify a cleansing of the spirit and a dedication to that which is good. Another part of me winced at the sight of the silly looking dog head on his oversized T-shirt, bobbing with each step until it was finally completely gone.

The pastor tipped Zachary back (his sister couldn't afford the bribe for the longer version), and when the pastor brought Zach back up, I clapped, I shouted, and I cried. Zach's hair was slick and stuck to his head, his ears poked out, his eyes were big and dark. He reminded me a lot of Frisket!

Zach wiped the water from his eyes, smiled at everyone clapping for him, and walked back up the steps. His oversized shirt was clinging and dripping, and when he turned from the top of the steps to look back, I couldn't help but smile at the little mousy-looking face on the front of his shirt.

I heard some whispering behind me as they read Zach's shirt: "*¡Yo quiero, Jesus!* I want Jesus." That's what Zach was saying that night. Suddenly I wished Frisket were there. I'm not sure, but it just seemed that would be right.

I have lots of stuff in my house that is there only because it reminds me of something else. An old, tattered quilt hangs on a rack in my bedroom to remind me of my grandmother. A small jar containing water I took from the Jordan River reminds me of my trip to Israel. And now there's Frisket.

Frisket finally has learned to leap up onto the couch without hurting herself. She still wants everyone and anyone to rub her belly, and her hipbones are *supposed* to look that way (I even asked the vet). She still curls up next to Zachary for bedtime, and every time a Taco Bell commercial comes on, Zach still holds her nose up close to the TV so she can get a good look at her cousin. I still think she looks like a mouse, and sometimes when I catch just a glimpse of her out of the corner of my eye, my heart skips a beat.

But now I see a side of Frisket I hadn't seen before—especially after we give her a bath, when her hair is all wet and slicked down. Her eyes seem to be bigger and her ears wider. That's probably when she looks the most like a big, white, laboratory rat. But that's also when she reminds me of my son the day he was baptized, the day he was cleansed, and the day he wanted all around him to know it. The day he said, "I want Jesus!"

chapter
6

Momma's Big Knife

> If anyone does not provide for his relatives, and
> especially for his immediate family, he has
> denied the faith and is worse than an unbeliever.
>
> 1 TIMOTHY 5:8

I'll never forget the day Momma stabbed my husband at the
indoor putt-putt place.

It all started one bright, spring morning when we left
Nashville in a rental van and headed for Branson, Missouri,
about a nine-hour drive. I was working close to Branson, and
since we had never been there before, we thought we would
head up a day early to see what the big hubbub about that
city was.

Mom and Sammy (her husband) had never been either,
so Sammy took a few days off from the plant, and Mom

found someone to fill in for her at the prison infirmary. That's why we had the van. We rented an extra-long one and took out the middle seat so there would be more room for the kids and so Momma could stretch out and take a nap.

David wasn't all that thrilled about taking a long trip with the in-laws. As a matter of fact, he's never been very big on driving across town with the in-laws let alone across the state border. (I think I'd read about some Mother-in-Law Syndrome while I was at college, and I was sure that's what he suffered from.)

Mom didn't help matters when she popped open the Tupperware just as we hit the highway and announced she had brought along something to snack on. The aroma of deviled eggs filled the van like one of those bug bombs. No matter how much you might like eggs, deviled eggs in a crowded van could be fatal.

David almost turned around and canceled the trip right then and there.

The first day we drove more than six hours (a lot of it with the windows down) and stayed just on the other side of St. Louis. To save money, we shared a room that had two beds and a couch (but only one bathroom). Mom brought the eggs in from the van so they would be handy if anyone wanted a midnight snack.

We finally made it into Branson the next afternoon, but all the theaters, most of the restaurants, and nearly all the souvenir shops were closed. Our waitress at the Waffle House told us the "season" didn't start until Saturday—that's when the place would be hopping. Since this was Wednesday, and we had to leave the next day, we would miss all the excitement.

David just sat there, twirling the van keys on his finger, not saying anything. We were surrounded by the smell of eggs cooked half a dozen different ways, and Branson didn't seem like such a hot place after all.

"Is *anything* open?" I asked the waitress (before the Waffle House Syndrome could set in).

"I think Funland's open," she said, pouring us more coffee. "They got some rides and games there—putt-putt too."

"I love putt-putt," said Sammy.

"Me and Sammy both love putt-putt," added Mom. "Y'all wanna play?"

David looked at me, and I gave him one of those don't-you-dare-hurt-Momma's-feelings looks. I could tell how hard it was for him to bite his tongue, but he did, and instead of something mean or cruel, he said, "Only if you bring along what's left of those deviled eggs."

Momma giggled and slapped Sammy on the arm. "Oh, this is gonna be so fun. What color ball do you want? Green or red? I want purple if they have it."

Funland's indoor putt-putt was open, just as the woman had said, so we all picked out our clubs and colored balls. Momma teed up and was preparing to strike her purple ball down a long fairway that did a loop-the-loop about halfway down when suddenly she stood up straight, letting her purse slip off her shoulder. She caught it by the strap and held it out for Sammy. "Honey, can you hold this? I wished I'd left it in the van."

"There's plenty of room in the van," Sammy said.

My purse was feeling sort of heavy too, so I handed mine to David and said, with my sweetest smile, "Honey, would you mind taking our purses to the van?"

Momma's Big Knife

David rolled his eyes, left his putter with me, and took off with the purses. We didn't see him again until we were at the windmill by hole nine. He limped up to the tee box, looking as white as a brand-new Titleist.

"What's wrong?" I asked, as he sat down on a plastic turtle's back.

"I've been stabbed." He pointed to his right shin.

I noticed a small hole in his jeans, circled in blood. "Who? How?"

With a trembling hand, he pointed to Mother, who only a few moments before had lost her purple ball beneath the windmill. Sammy was on his hands and knees trying to run it out with his putter. Mom was leaning over him and giving instructions.

"To the left, Sammy. No, the right. Look out! Here comes the windmill!" And Sammy would have to scurry backward like a crab to keep from getting sliced in two by the windmill blades.

"Tell me *how* Mom stabbed you," I said to David.

As David talked, he bent over and rolled up his pant leg to expose a nasty wound that was bleeding a lot. "It wasn't really her but her purse. As I went out the swinging door, the door swung back and hit me and the purse, and the big knife your mom's carrying around in her purse went right through the bag and into my leg."

The blood was making me queasy. I stood up and called to Mom, "Mom, why do you have a big knife in your purse?"

Mom told Sammy to keep looking while she answered, "It's a paring knife, honey. You know, in case the children would want me to peel an apple for them." She had given Sammy her putter and now directed him to use both of them under the windmill—like giant wiper blades.

Throughout the rest of the game, Zach and Chera had more fun looking at the hole in their father's leg than at the holes they were supposed to be putting into. Mom was a bit upset that she wasn't able to find her purple ball but seemed better when she was able to finish with David's yellow one—since he wasn't playing now anyway.

After Mom putted the ball at the last hole into the hippo's mouth, she rolled up her sleeves and went to work on David. At first he was a bit reluctant, and I couldn't blame him (but I wasn't going to frisk my own mother!). "You're forgetting I'm a prison nurse," she said. "I've seen a few of these."

So David handed over his leg, and Mom patched him up.

Something happened that day in Branson—besides the free game of putt-putt Mom won when she hit the hippo's mouth. I think I remember reading something about this when I was in school—the Florence Nightingale Syndrome or something, in which the patient and the nurse draw closer together because of all the blood, pain, bandages, and stuff. Even after we left Branson, spending a few more days in Arkansas, the only person David would let "baby" his wound was Mom. "Let her do it," he would say through teeth clenched in pain whenever I'd try to spread on some medicine. "She does this sort of stuff all the time."

Then the two of them would have this conversation: "Have you seen worse?" "Is it infected?" "Ever see anyone die from a wound like this?" I'd never heard them talk so much before.

To be honest, once we washed away the dried blood from David's leg, all we could see was a tiny cut that didn't even impress Zachary, who was four at the time. But I didn't say

Momma's Big Knife

anything to stop what was happening between my husband and my mother. I liked what I was seeing—and hearing.

"Hey," he called out once while driving down the interstate, "there's a rest stop up ahead. Wake up your mom and get her to check my bandages, will you? I think my toes are starting to go numb."

There are those in this world we love to just hang out with, but sometimes it takes a tragedy to make us forget our differences and to pull us close together as we fight for a common cause. After Mom stabbed David, the two formed a bond as they swapped bloody stories, spread Neosporin, and wrapped gauze. Because of what happened in Branson— at the putt-putt place—I see that the best place to meet someone, to talk, to connect, is on common ground, a place that surely exists between any two people, no matter how different they might be. I pray that I will always recognize that moment and that place (without the inconvenience of being stabbed, of course).

A Close Blush with the Law

> For all have sinned and fall short of the glory of God, and are justified freely by his grace through the redemption that came by Christ Jesus.
>
> ROMANS 3:23–24

We were on our way to church when the police officer pulled us over—doing 69 in a 50-miles-per-hour zone. David was driving, and I had told him just seconds before the siren blared out that he was going way too fast.

"Mom, what's going to happen?" Zachary, then ten, wanted to know, straining against his seatbelt to see the strobing blue lights.

"Your father is going to get a ticket for speeding," I told Zach. "He was going way too fast and was breaking the law, and he deserves a ticket. So just sit back and keep quiet."

David groaned and slowed down to pull over, being careful to use his turn signal.

"Just tell them who you are, Mom," Zach said. "If he knows you're a famous comedian, maybe he won't give you a ticket."

"I'm not a famous comedian, Zach. And besides, I don't think that will work."

I'm sure Zach was thinking that because I'd been on television a few times I was famous. I do get recognized every once in a while at the oddest times, like when my mouth is full of steamed rice, or when I'm getting my hair fixed and the hairdresser has just put one of those clear plastic bags over my head. That's when people will come up to me and say, "Why, I think I've seen you on television, haven't I?"

David hadn't said a word so far, but then again, he usually doesn't when he is angry. He just gets real quiet, his lips get real thin, and his face gets real red. He looked like that now.

"Honey, please don't say a word to the officer," I said. "You were wrong, and you deserve whatever you get. Besides, the children are watching, and I believe this is a good time to teach them about the consequences of breaking the law."

David turned to give me the look I've seen him give our sixteen-year-old daughter, Chera, whenever she turns the stereo up too loud—just a look, not a word. Face red. Lips thin. Breathing hard.

The officer walked up to the side of the van and asked for David's license. David pulled it from his wallet without saying a word and handed it to the officer. The guy was an older man, late fifties or early sixties, and the hair sticking out from beneath his big, blue hat was gray.

"Son," he said in a gravelly voice, "do you know how fast you were going?"

"Sixty?"

"Sixty-nine!"

"Sixty-five, maybe."

"Sixty-nine!"

"Sixty-nine?! I'm pretty sure I was only—"

"That's a $150 fine," said the officer. "Did you know that?" He was holding David's license in his hand and looking at David, checking the picture. Then he looked at me, then back to David, and then to me. I straightened my dress because the seatbelt was wrinkling it. Now he was staring straight at me. Slowly his eyes widened, he smiled, and he said, "Chonda Pierce? Is that you?"

I leaned over and squinted at the nametag on his chest. "John Holder?"

"Yeah!"

"Well, how have you been?" I asked, blushing.

He reached across David and shook my hand and just laughed and laughed. He asked about Momma, wanted to know how she was doing and if she had remarried.

I knew John Holder from way back. For as long as I could remember, he owned one of the two full-service gas stations in town, complete with a wrecker service on the side. After my older sister, Charlotta, was in an accident that killed her almost twenty-three years before, his wrecker company went out and picked up her car. Mom used to stop at his gas station to fill up the car and get her windshield washed, and he would always ask about how she was doing and about my sister Cheralyn and me. My dad invited John Holder to church, and he came and I saw him sing hymns.

A Close Blush with the Law

I used to think he was such a hard man with his sharp chin and bony cheeks. But then I saw him at Cheralyn's funeral less than two years after Charlotta's accident. And after I saw him weep, I didn't think that way anymore. For a few years after that, whenever Mom would go to Ashland City and run into him, he would always ask about me. Whenever I ran into him, he would ask about Momma. Yes, I knew John Holder from way back.

I think somewhere along the way I'd even heard that he had been elected police chief of this small town. I guess that was true because it said so on his nametag. And now here he was pulling us over for doing 69 in a 50-miles-per-hour zone.

I introduced him to my children, and he reached back and shook Chera and Zachary's hands. I introduced him to David, and David started to shake his hand when Officer Holder pointed at him with the license and said sternly, "Listen, you have to slow down. One, $150 is an expensive fine. And two," John Holder pointed to my two children buckled up in back. "You have a couple of babies there that I'm sure you don't want anything to happen to." He looked at me and nodded, as if to say he and I knew all about bad car wrecks.

David let his hand drop to the window, sort of embarrassed, and looked away.

"Now, take this." John Holder handed David his license back. "And you *slow down*."

David took the license, and I was so glad he only nodded. But then he said, "I played baseball with your son, Danny."

John Holder looked at David and thought for a moment. "Yeah, yeah, Danny played baseball. Now you slow down.

Understand?" Then he looked at me and smiled and said, "It's so good to see you again, Chonda. Please tell your momma I said hello."

"I will," I said. "And do come to church sometime. That's where we're headed."

He smiled back. "You know, I really will. I've always liked that church." And I knew what he was talking about—about my sisters' funerals, about my dad, my mom, the revivals, about feeling God's presence so much John Holder would weep and wouldn't care who saw him. I knew that's what he was talking about.

David waited until John Holder drove off before putting the van into gear and proceeding down the road much slower than he had before.

"See, Mom," Zachary said with a laugh. "If you tell them who you are, you won't get a ticket."

"Now, Zachary, that's not how it happens *all* the time." I was glad I had seen my old friend John Holder, but I was a bit flustered that my object lesson about facing up to the consequences of your actions had fallen through. "If you do wrong, you always pay a price. This time we . . . we . . ." I was trying to decide which way to go here ". . . we just got *lucky*. When you do something wrong and get off scot-free like that, it's just—"

"Grace," David said.

I looked over at him and watched him drop his license into his suit coat pocket. He wasn't red faced or thin lipped any more. He was breathing easier and smiling—not a smug little smile like you see on a person's face who believes he just got away with something, but a smile that seemed to express relief, a pleasant smile. He smiled like someone who knew he should have been punished but wasn't; someone who should have been fined severely but hadn't been; someone who should have had to pay a big price but didn't.

"Grace," he said again. "Why don't you tell the children about grace?"

Manhattan Takes Us

So is my word that goes out from my mouth: It
will not return to me empty, but will accomplish
what I desire and achieve the purpose for which
I sent it.

ISAIAH 55:11

A few years ago, David and I went to New York City for
the first time. I had to work for two days, and then we had a
day and a night to sightsee—and did we ever!

We took a cab from the airport to our hotel on Times
Square. Our cab driver spoke a lot of Spanish, or maybe it
was Arabic, or French—all I know is that he spoke "some"
English.

"Is that the Empire State Building?" David asked the
driver, pointing to a tall building while clinging to the car's
little strap on which one could hang dry cleaning.

"No, no, Empire St—HEY! WATCH WHERE YOU'RE GOING, YOU $#%$&*!" Our driver lambasted the guy in the cab next to us. Then he veered so close to the other car that David and I both scooted to the opposite side of the car. Our driver wiped his brow and said, "Empire State Building is—FOR THE LOVE OF . . . WHERE DID YOU LEARN TO DRIVE, YOU @$%&*!!?" He swerved back the other way, and David and I scooted back over to the other side of the car. Then he addressed us. "Maybe if you look—" Then back to our neighbor, "FOR CRYING OUT LOUD! YOU @$%&*#!" He used plenty of facial expressions and hand gestures that seemed to work in all languages.

"That's okay," David said. "We'll see it soon, I'm sure. I mean, it's giant, right? Can't miss it." He twisted his hand in the little strap and closed his eyes. I hung on to him tightly, since there were no air bags in the backseat.

Once we arrived at our hotel, David helped to pull the bags from the trunk, took a look around Times Square, and said, "Wow! So *this* is where Dick Clark hangs out."

We really were in New York City!

The first thing David said the next day as we set out to take Manhattan was, "Let's go to Central Park."

"Why?" I wanted to know, when Macy's and Saks Fifth Avenue were so close and so big.

"Because it's famous," he answered. "In all the movies, that's the place everybody goes—spies, kidnappers, joggers. They go to feed the pigeons and meet. We have to see that."

On our map Central Park looked to be only about five blocks away, so we set out on foot. We quickly learned not to cross any streets unless the picture of the walking man on

the crossing light was lit up. In only three blocks I saved David's life three times, and he saved mine twice.

As we walked, we stopped once to watch people ice skate on an outdoor rink.

"Wow, this is big and nice." David waved an arm out over the giant rink. "I wonder what this is?"

We looked for a sign. "There it is," I said. "Rockefeller Plaza. That sounds familiar."

David nodded. "Maybe he was a famous ice skater. You know, Olympics or something."

"Maybe," I said, and we moved on.

When we finally reached Central Park, I saw what it was I wanted to do. "Let's take a carriage ride. That will be so romantic."

David winced a bit, but we found an empty one and the woman driver told us we could just pay her at the end of the ride whatever we thought the ride was worth. I saw David pull a five-dollar bill from his wallet, fold it, and slip it into his pocket—getting ready. Before we climbed in, he tapped me on the shoulder and pointed to an old, gray-haired man sitting on a park bench, feeding the pigeons.

"He's probably a Russian spy," David said.

"And this carriage is probably bugged," I added as I climbed in. David didn't say anything, but now he seemed nervous.

The ride was going great. Trees were turning springtime green, flowers were blooming, and our guide wasn't saying very much, just letting us enjoy the ride. Then David asked, "Hey, isn't that the bridge where that *Home Alone* kid met the pigeon lady?"

"Yes, it is." Just like that, our guide had David figured out, and she started to work for her tip. "And if you look right over there," she said, pointing with her whip above some trees, "that top balcony on the end is Madonna's place."

"Really?" said David.

"Oh, yeah. And over there," and she pointed to another tall building with balconies, "that's Arnold Schwarzenegger's place."

"No!"

She nodded. "Three point four million dollars."

"Wow!"

Our carriage turned a corner, and she pointed to a brownstone building that we could see only for a second through an opening in the trees. "And that's where John Lennon was shot."

David punched me in the arm and pointed too, to make sure I didn't miss that.

Before we circled back to where we had started, past a tulip bed that was as colorful as a bowl of jelly beans, we also saw where the car chase in *Die Hard II* was shot and where Crocodile Dundee slept. Some romantic ride.

At the end of the ride, David fished out his wallet, paid our guide fifty bucks, and asked for directions to the Empire State Building.

We had a long way to walk, so we agreed it was time for a bathroom break. "Where will we find a restroom?" I asked him.

We stood on the busy sidewalk, and David scanned the skyline. He pointed to the golden building across the street and said, "There. That'll be perfect."

So we took a ten-minute potty break at the Trump Tower. It was very nice. Lots of marble, lots of mirrors.

On our way to the Empire State Building we stumbled across the New York Public Library, and David had to go in.

"This will be even more romantic than the carriage ride," he predicted.

"The Trump Tower was more romantic than the carriage ride," I said, but I don't think he heard me.

Up the long steps and past the concrete lions that guarded the way, we entered the library, where a special exhibit so captivated us we used up most of our shopping time. (I know, I know that's hard to believe.) But what we saw there would prove to be worth it; what we saw there ended up knocking all the rough edges off the rest of a crazy day.

Right after we left the library, we made it to the Empire State Building, where we stood in front of it looking straight up for the longest time.

"Wow!" David said.

I was thinking that this was where Tom Hanks met Meg Ryan in *Sleepless in Seattle* (now that was romantic!), and I was about to ask David what he was thinking when suddenly he said, "If you spit off the top, I wonder how long it would take to reach the sidewalk."

I tried to ignore him.

The top of the building is a lot different than it looks in the movies. For one thing, a big metal fence goes all the way around so you can't lean over to see how tiny everyone looks. But for a quarter we did take turns peering through a telescope at the Statue of Liberty.

After eating Empire State Building burgers from the first-floor grill, we headed back to Times Square because we had tickets to a comedy club for later. And that's when I saw it.

"Macy's!" I cried out, grabbing David's hand and leading him through the front door as he kicked and screamed.

Someone at the front door told us, "I'm sorry, but we close in thirty minutes." *No problem*, I thought. We zipped through Macy's in a New York minute.

We found one section in which everything was ugly and expensive, and David kept reading aloud the prices of the dresses, "$4,000, $7,000, $8,000!"

"Just give me a stapler and that old quilt of your grandmother's and I can make this." He pointed to a crazy-patterned dress.

As we were leaving, we started to pass by a man who was dressed like a king. At first I thought maybe he was an actor from Broadway—maybe from *The King and I* or . . . "What's another famous king show?" I asked David.

"King Kong," he shot back.

I ignored David. Although this king wasn't apelike, neither was he bald like Yul Brenner. He was holding a tiny glass bottle that had one of those squeeze pumps on top. The king flapped the tails of his robe, took a step toward David, flashed this big smile, and asked David if he would like to smell like a prince. Before David could say a word, the king doused him in a cloud that was very light, airy, and sweet. David was so shocked that he staggered away from the king as if he had been shot with an arrow rather than *Eau du Prince*. David tried to rub it off his neck, but that didn't work, and we were too far away to walk to the Trump Tower, where there was plenty of soap and water.

Escaping the perfume purveyor to the great outdoors, we discovered it was nighttime now, but it sure wasn't dark on Times Square. "This place is lit up like a Christmas tree." David looked about as if he were counting the bulbs.

We stopped for a moment next to a small stage where a huge, muscular black man wearing a spiked collar was reading from the Bible. David put his arm around my shoulders and said, "Wow, listen. He's preaching the Word." Soon another man, who was wearing a big chain looped from his nose to his ear, joined the man with the spiked collar.

"Ouch! That's got to be uncomfortable," David said, probably a little louder than necessary, as he rubbed the end of his own nose. "That reminds me," he said, "is someone checking on the dogs back home?"

I ignored him because now every time the man with the spiked collar came to the end of a sentence, the man with the chain in his nose would pound his fist into his palm.

Before long a nice-sized crowd had gathered behind us, and David and I were suddenly in the front row, trying to be supportive of the young pastors. Not until the man with the spiked collar began to shout about how the white man was to blame for all the pain in the world did we figure we weren't exactly in the middle of a love feast.

We tried to slip out quietly and unobserved, but a lot of eyes followed us, and I thought I could hear a chain rattle behind us. As we passed by some of the other listeners, I also noticed a few of them sniffing the air as David—smelling like a prince—scampered past.

On the way to the comedy club, we stayed close together, crossing streets only when the lights said so and trying not to look at anyone else—even the man who passed us with a bloody nose. But David couldn't help it, and he looked way too long. The bloody man got up in David's face and shouted, "Are you looking at my nose?"

David paused and said, "Ah, there's a fine bathroom at the Trump—"

I yanked on David's arm, and we ran off like two kids chasing the school bus.

At the comedy club, we ordered this taco-like thing from the menu and discovered it was huge. It was also terrible. We picked at it a bit and talked about getting room service later—that is, if we could make it back to the hotel alive.

The comedy that night was okay, but the funniest thing that happened was when a waitress dropped some glasses and they shattered. Pieces of broken glass bounced up and landed right into our taco-something. Our waitress then brought us another heaping portion of the stuff we already hated—"at no extra charge."

We made it back to the hotel late—but alive. I called room service and ordered way too much, but it had been a long, long day. Our sightseeing adventure had put us eyeball-to-eyeball with sights we never could have imagined—not even for New York. I'll never forget our cab ride into the city, the king with the perfume bottle, the preacher with the dog collar, or the man with the bloody nose.

But what struck me most about that day was our time in the New York Public Library. You see, that happened to be the month of the Tyndale Bible Exhibit. So when we walked into the cool, quiet building from the noisy, pushy sidewalks, God's words, bold and bright, were right there on the wall in big block letters:

> But they that wait upon the LORD shall renew their strength; they shall mount up with wings as eagles; they shall run, and not be weary; and they shall walk, and not faint.
>
> —Isaiah 40:31 (KJV)

The room in the library was dark except for the words on the wall and the open Bibles displayed around the room. These areas were bright and glowing, the words there for all to read. To me, in the library's quiet, those words were louder than anything I had heard that day, more impressive than Macy's Department Store or Arnold Schwarzenneger's penthouse apartment.

My prayer is that in the craziness and busyness of life, whether in New York City or in my small Tennessee town, God's Word can be found in the center, in the heart—and all lit up like a Christmas tree!

The Great Diaper Derby

> Consider how the lilies grow. They do not labor or spin. Yet I tell you, not even Solomon in all his splendor was dressed like one of these. If that is how God clothes the grass of the field, which is here today, and tomorrow is thrown into the fire, how much more will he clothe you, O you of little faith!
>
> LUKE 12:27–28

At one point in time David and I believed that if we had a two-week supply of diapers, everything would be just great. So imagine our surprise when we discovered, while strolling through the mall one evening, a baby race that provided the winner with a two-weeks' supply of disposable diapers—and not those cheap, store-brand kind that gave Chera diaper rash.

David held Chera in his arms while I filled out an entry form. "Are you sure she's up to this?" I asked. After all, she was only fifteen months old. But David reminded me that she had started to walk at nine months, so she had a good six months' experience.

When we finished the paperwork, we were given a big, sticky number four that we stuck to the back of her tiny shirt. We were directed to the far end of a cushy mat that was about fifteen feet long and divided into six lanes by white stripes.

I heard David talking to Chera about "visualizing victory" and "running like a gazelle." But all I could think of was what if my little baby ran over the white line, bumped noggins with another runner, and knocked loose the only tooth she had—the one we were so proud of. If she lost the race, would she be traumatized forever? Was the mat soft enough? Had they used a disinfectant to clean it after the last race? Did anyone think about cleaning it at all?

A young woman (who was surely way too young to have children of her own) wearing a ponytail and chewing gum explained the race's rules. "First of all, I'd like to welcome all of you to the Great Diaper Derby here at Hickory Hollow Mall. Since I don't speak baby language—hee hee—let me explain to the contestants' parents how this race is supposed to go. To start out, one parent will stand at this end of the mat with your child in your respective lane." She pointed to the end of the mat where we already were standing. Each lane was marked with a number between one and six.

"The other parent is welcome to stand or sit at the finish line and call your child to you. You can call, clap, sing, whatever it takes, but do not touch or reach across the line to drag your child across."

It was time to take our positions, so David finished massaging Chera's legs (while she giggled) and took his place at the finish line. He got on his hands and knees and made faces at her, causing her to giggle more. She tried to squirm from my arms to run to him, and David called back, "Oh, that's good. That's real good, Chera. Channel that! Channel that!"

We had stripped Chera down to just a diaper and a shirt—no shoes or socks on the mat, David had said. "That'll only slow her down. She needs to feel the wind between her toes."

I tightly held on to Chera and waited for the girl with the gum and ponytail to start the race. That gave me a chance to size up the competition. After a quick look around, I began to think my baby just might win this thing. "Run like a gazelle!" I wanted to shout but decided not to.

We were in lane four. Next to us, on the far left in lanes one and two, were twin boys with big, curly hair. They were both sitting—despite what their hairless father kept shouting at them from the finish line. One was even chewing on the end of his shoe and therefore wasn't positioned for a quick start. Racer number three was crying and trying to get her mom to pick her up. Her mom kept pushing her back down and telling her to run like she did at home whenever Grandpa would take out his teeth and try to bite her with them. But the thought of that just made the toddler cry even more.

In lane five was a contestant who couldn't even walk yet—or if she could, she preferred to crawl. (Earlier I had noticed that whenever she crawled to a wall or table, her mom would pick her up and point her in the right direction, as if she were a box turtle.) Finally, in lane six was a child with a very runny nose, *very* runny.

The girl with the ponytail and chewing gum shouted, "On your marks!"

The Great Diaper Derby

I wanted to call time-out and wipe racer number six's nose myself.

"Get set!"

I whispered in Chera's ear, "Run to Daddy when I say so, Chera." She was already squirming and trying to pull free.

"Go!"

I let go, and Chera bolted down the mat like a . . . *like a gazelle!* David was red faced and calling her to him, fanning the air, pulling Chera along in the draft. Her little, naked feet pitter-pattered across the germ-laden rubber mat, sounding like raindrops. She was only two steps away from the finish line when I realized how badly I wanted those diapers, when I realized that this was how God was going to provide for us. "Go, Chera! Go! Run like the—"

She stopped.

And the wind stuck in my throat, as all I could do was watch. David's arm kept pinwheeling, creating a breeze that blew back his hair, but Chera would not budge. Instead, she stood there and stared at her father (probably at the little blue vein that pops up on his forehead whenever he gets excited).

"Come on to Daddy," David grunted, his arm spinning at the shoulder joint like a puppet's. "Come across this line for your surprise! Come on. I'll give you a piece of candy. How about some ice cream? Wouldn't you like some ice cream? Come on across the line. No more naps—ever! Just cross the line!"

David was starting to embarrass me. In the meantime, the twins were off and running; however, they opted to run diagonally. The one that had been chewing on his shoe earlier led the way for a bit. But his shoelace had come untied and he stepped on it, tripping into lane three and sliding all the way to lane five. His brother was right behind him, and together they wound up in lane six—crying. Their hairless father was jangling his car keys in hopes that would attract them, but the one who had found his shoe earlier found it again and began to chew.

The crying girl in lane three who wanted her mommy never did get going. In fact, she just cried louder and louder. Her dad had even pulled an Oreo cookie from his pocket and was waggling it in the air. This only made her cry more.

The runny-nosed kid nearly got us both disqualified when he made a beeline for Chera. With arms pulled back, shoulders raised, and (runny) nose first, he took at least a dozen baby steps toward Chera and was about to crash into her (doctor's bills, antibiotics—I could see it all coming) when he suddenly veered off toward the Oreo cookie that was meant for the crying racer who only wanted her mommy. He blindsided the father and snatched away the cookie.

Well, this only made the crying kid in lane three more furious, and she wailed so loud that I couldn't hear David on the other end, but I *could* read his lips. "Come on, Chera. I'll give you a car! A house! Half of my kingdom!"

But Chera wouldn't budge. She just stood there, two steps from crossing the line, and stared at David, who I was afraid would pass out—if not that, he was in the process of giving away everything we ever owned (and a lot we didn't) for the sake of two weeks' worth of diapers.

In the midst of the screaming, the fanning, the cookies, the snot, and the teething, one little baby moved steadily forward on all fours, past the crying baby in lane three, past the twins (who were both chewing on their own—and each other's—shoes and had sprawled out in lanes four, five, and six), past the runny-nosed kid, who now had a combination of snot and Oreos all over his face, and even past Chera, who could have been a statue placed there to face her father. The little child who crawled everywhere crawled right up into her father's arms and began to pull at his nose. I watched the father hold his baby and close his eyes—probably dreaming of that two-weeks' supply of diapers stacked in a corner of the baby's room.

With the race over, David reached out and gathered Chera in his arms and began to talk to her. The big vein in his forehead had returned to normal, and his face wasn't as red. I walked up and heard him saying to her, "Shake it off. You'll get 'em next time. Hey, you can't win 'em all."

I put Chera's socks and shoes back on her feet as quickly as I could and noticed that no one was disinfecting the mat to prepare for the next race.

On the way home David stopped at 7-11 and bought us all ice cream cones and Chera a pack of diapers, enough to last her about four days. To pay for the diapers, he would have to work about two hours and probably would have to get pretty greasy. (He was a heating and air conditioning mechanic.)

It seemed like such an easy way to meet our needs, I thought. *Win the race and get free diapers.* I tried to make myself think that maybe the crawling baby from lane number five needed them more than we did.

For a couple of days I wondered why God hadn't met our needs when we had given him such an easy opportunity to do so. But only for a couple of days, because after that it turned cold and pipes all over town froze and burst. David worked lots of overtime, enough to buy lots and lots of diapers—and we did.

God always has met our needs, but rarely in the ways I think he will or even should. But after all, he is God, and he has great plans for his children—crying ones, whiny ones, fast ones, slow ones, and ones with runny noses—and his plans don't always include winning a Great Diaper Derby in the mall.

The Dog That Ate My Living Room

> For I am convinced that neither death nor life,
> neither angels nor demons, neither the present
> nor the future, nor any powers, neither height nor
> depth, nor anything else in all creation, will be
> able to separate us from the love of God that is
> in Christ Jesus our Lord.
>
> ROMANS 8:38–39

I wanted to kill that dog the first week we had him (which must be the terrible twos in dog years), but I didn't—but only for the children's sake.

My daughter, Chera, was eight years old when Disney did a remake of the movie *101 Dalmatians*. That Christmas she wanted a dalmatian more than anything else in the world. Neither David nor I was too thrilled about something that eats and you-know-whats, but we figured a puppy would be easier to find than a Cabbage Patch doll.

Of course, I should have known when we picked out the puppy that he was going to be trouble because the owner kept telling us how this was the last one of ten brothers and sisters. Why had everyone else skipped over him?

Since this was a Christmas present from Santa, David and I brought the pup home under cover of darkness.

"Maybe you can sing to him or something," said the woman who sold him to us. "To calm him down, since he's never ridden in a car."

I held the little freckled thing in my lap, wrapped in a blanket, and could feel him trembling through the covers. So as David drove, I began to sing, "You are my sunshine, my only sunshine." (It had worked for my son, Zachary, when *he* was two.)

The road back to our house was curvy, and one minute we were all leaning to the right, then we would straighten up, and then lean to the left. I was just singing about "how I had held you in my arms" when the little fellow bolted from my arms and landed on the dark floorboard where I couldn't see a thing but could feel him squirming around.

"Oops, he got away," I said.

"What do you mean, 'He got away'?" David asked. "He's in the car, isn't he?"

"Yes, but I mean I don't have him." I was groping in the black. "Turn on the light. He's somewhere down—"

"What's that smell?" asked David.

Then there came the loudest retching noise I'd ever heard from man or beast (and I have an older brother).

"Yuck! What's that smell?" David pulled onto the shoulder of the road and turned on the inside lights.

We found the tiny puppy standing there at my feet, trembling, surrounded by . . . well, let's just say everything was green and brown. David used an old piece of cardboard to clean up, although a shovel would have been better.

Not only did the new puppy get carsick, but he also was a whiner. We closed him off in the laundry room with a nice, soft bed and plenty of water and food. But every time we would walk away, he would whine.

"Shush," David begged. "Santa's coming tonight. Don't you want to be a good boy? Maybe Santa will bring you something." Not even the promise of goodies from the North Pole would shut up the dog. But when David went into the room to be with him, the puppy would lick his hand and stop whining.

"Oh," I said, "looks like he just wants to be with you."

"I could bring him to bed," David suggested.

"Or you could stay here with him," I voted.

So David slept on the floor in the laundry room on Christmas Eve—probably with visions of sugarplums dancing in his head. I tiptoed off to bed, and I heard him exclaim, as I walked out of sight, "What's that awful smell?!"

On Christmas morning David got up all red eyed, his hair sticking out crazylike, but he had the video camera on his shoulder and was ready to go. When the children came racing down the steps, the little dalmatian raced in a blur up the steps and right past them.

"What was that?" Chera wanted to know.

"It was a puppy!" Zach, who was four, cried out. "It was a puppy!"

They got to the bottom of the stairs and called the puppy. David kept the video rolling.

The Dog That Ate My Living Room

"What's he doing up there?" David asked.

Zach stood where he could peek up the stairs and answered, "Pee-peeing."

David grumbled.

"Come here!" Chera sang. "Come here ... uh ... boy? Girl?"

"Boy," David answered through his teeth.

"Come here, boy," Chera called out in her high-pitched voice and clapped her hands. The puppy raced and tumbled down the steps and landed right on Chera's chest, knocking her back and licking her face.

Zach petted him and said, "What's that smell?"

Right away Chera began to talk puppy talk, and the puppy seemed to understand. "Oh, you a good boyee. Yes, you are. Look at the little puppy. Oooooo! You such a happy puppy. Yes, you are. You like to lick my nose, don't you?"

"Ooo. He licked her nose!" cried Zach.

For the rest of the morning the puppy bounced around the house, up the stairs, down the stairs, under the tree, and over and through the mounds of wrapping paper. David followed him around with a wet cloth and some spray cleaner.

That night we watched *101 Dalmatians* (another of Chera's Christmas presents), and those puppies in the movie seemed so cute. They sat when they were supposed to, they ran where they were supposed to, and no one ever talked about how funny they smelled.

"So what are you going to name him?" I asked Chera after the movie was over. "How about Freckles? Or Pepper? Like in the movie." But Chera didn't seem to like either of those.

"Well, we have to call him something besides 'Hey, boy,'" I pointed out.

"Naming a dog takes time," said David, holding a wet cloth. "The name has to fit, has to be just right—just right for Chera and . . . Hey Boy. Me? I'd call him Leaky. But that's me. She'll come up with something that fits."

The dog almost didn't live long enough to be named. In the movie, the dalmatians chewed up only the bad people's stuff, and everyone would clap and laugh at how clever they were. Our dog (Chewy would have been a good name) ate everything. When we went out, we left him closed up in the laundry room with plenty of food, water, and a bed, but that wasn't good enough for him. He chewed through the louvered door and went after the couch (Couch-Eater would have been another good name). He chewed off the sofa's front legs so that, when we arrived home, the couch had tilted forward and was lying facedown on the floor—dead. Couch-Eater had a cushion between his paws. That would have gone next, I'm sure, had we not interrupted.

During the next couple of weeks, the dog tore up a chunk of carpet (Carpet Chomper, maybe), scratched the linoleum in the bathroom (Linoleum Gouger), and ate the baseboard in the upstairs hallway (Baseboard Muncher). I still don't know how he did that last one.

Then the day came when we were ready to move—to a house with a yard where we could drive a stake deep into the ground and tie on a chain. "Bet he can't eat through that!" David said as he marched off to the hardware store to prepare our present home for sale. He came home with wood patch, carpet patch, a louver replacement kit, and a big throw rug to cover the hole in the living room. We stacked bricks

The Dog That Ate My Living Room

under the front of the sofa, and then decided to abandon it. "Or we could take it along and let Hey Boy use it as a chew toy," David suggested.

"I've got it!" Chera told us one day.

"Got what?" I asked.

"Got a name for him," she said, pointing to the spotted dog stretched out on his sofa, which barely was balanced on a couple of bricks.

"How about Smelly?" asked Zach, holding his nose.

"How about SPOT?" Chera said.

"Spot?" I asked.

"Spot?" David asked.

"I get it!" said Zach. "Because he has spots!"

"No," said Chera. "Not Spot. S-P-O-T. SPOT. You told me, Dad, that his father's name was Sir Pepper. So we'll call him Sir Pepper Otis Theodore—SPOT!" She walked over and scratched the dog's belly, and he rolled over so she wouldn't miss a single spot. "Hey, SPOT," she said. "Do you like that name?"

From then on his name was SPOT.

SPOT liked his new yard. David bought a doghouse and let the kids paint SPOT above the door. He put up a fence, and SPOT ran in circles in the yard until he beat a path around the edges. Sometimes David would plant bushes and SPOT would dig them up. David would chase him around and around on the path the dog already had made. Sometimes SPOT would dig a hole under the fence and run off, and a neighbor would call to tell us that SPOT had just pottied on her bushes. Sometimes David called him names besides SPOT. I was sure that only confused the poor dog.

I Can See Myself in His Eyeballs

David and I could think of a dozen reasons we wanted to kill that dog. But then we had a couple of great reasons not to: Chera and Zachary. They loved that dog more than Nintendo and more than CDs. It didn't matter to them if SPOT chewed purses, dug holes, or tracked up the living room carpet. He could bark all night at a squirrel in a tree so that no one got any sleep, but they still loved that dog. We could go away for a week and come back in the middle of the night, and SPOT would jump up on the kids, lick their faces, and wag his tail. Zach would scratch him behind his ears, and Chera would talk her dog talk, and SPOT would talk back to her.

One day I realized that what was playing out before me was unconditional love: I love you, no strings attached, no matter what. Since then, whenever I need to be reminded about unconditional love, I just watch those three together.

I've learned in my own life that it doesn't matter what I may have messed up—even if I tracked through the living room with big, muddy footprints—God still loves me.

Unconditional Love, that would have been a good name for that crazy dog too. But I don't think the doghouse was big enough to paint the name on it.

Our Family Reunion in a Minivan

The LORD then said to Noah, "Go into the ark, you and your whole family."

GENESIS 7:1

I just wanted to get close again to my brother, Michael. I wanted to get closer to his wife, Doris, closer to their two boys (my nephews!), Josh, who was fourteen, and Jacob, who was eight. And I wanted David to get closer to them too, as well as Chera, who was eleven, and Zachary, who was five.

You see, while I was still in high school, Michael had gotten married and moved away, started a career, and had two sons, who now were growing up way too fast. For fifteen years he had been away from "home"—mostly in Ohio. So when an opportunity came up for us to spend a week together in Colorado, it seemed like an answer to my prayer for us all to get closer. Of course, the minivan helped a lot.

Doris played the piano for me during my performances, so the two of us flew into Denver from somewhere else, while David drove the minivan from Tennessee with the kids, picked up Mike and the boys, and planned three days of camping along the way to Colorado.

Once we all got together, we stayed for a whole week in one hotel room in Estes Park. David and I slept in one bed, Mike and Doris in another, Josh slept on the couch, and Chera, Zach, and Jacob camped out on the floor. The first night, as we all said goodnight to each other, Zach wanted to know what that funny smell was, and we all giggled and laughed. I fell asleep with a grin on my face. After all these years, it was so good to be this close to family again.

During the week, we hiked up a small mountain called Bible Point and talked to God. We picnicked in the mountains, saw deer and elk, and let the chipmunks eat out of our hands. Josh talked us into racing go-carts, and Mike and David learned to fly fish. One afternoon Mike hooked his ear really badly and bled all over himself, and then he and David both were run off from the kiddie pond, which was limited to fishing for fourteen-year-olds and younger. (They said they didn't see the sign.) When it was time to go back to Ohio, we crammed all our luggage, sleeping bags, tent, and bodies (all eight of them) into the minivan and drove through the mountains so we could see snow in August.

We got real close to elk, touched snow, sang songs, and even stopped at the peak for a cup of hot chocolate. But we were getting a bit cramped in the minivan, so we decided to cut the tour short and head home.

Mike said, "Let's try to make it to the other side of Denver, just about an hour, and get a hotel room—two of them this time." And he chuckled.

"I just want a nice, hot shower," said Doris.

"I have to stretch my legs." Josh was lying on top of the ice cooler that was wedged between the side door and the seat.

"I'm going to miss the chipmunks," said Chera.

"I drank way too much Dr. Pepper." David screwed up his face and held one hand to his stomach.

"What's that funny smell?" asked Zach.

Mike cracked his window a bit, and we drove on through the mountains toward Denver, with the setting sun painting the sky behind us.

I'll never forget the look on Michael's face as he came out of the hotel we had hoped we would sleep in that night. "They said they're full. Maybe if we go a little bit farther, closer to the state line, we'll find something."

David, who was driving, banged his head against the side window when he heard the news. Joshua groaned and crawled back onto the ice cooler. Doris said, "I still get the shower first." Chera and Jacob started a new alphabet game (they already had played at least a dozen) using road signs. Zach wanted to know what that funny smell was. But I was still enjoying the time with my family all packed in around me, and I told them so.

We drove on farther, nearly to the state line, and finally pulled off the interstate where about five different hotels were all lit up. From one to another we went, and the story was always the same: full, no room here, perhaps on into Kansas.

"Does anybody want to play the alphabet game?" asked Chera.

"I'm tired of that stupid game," said Jacob.

"It's not a stupid game."

"Is too."

"Is not."

"Is too."

"Children," I cut in, "let's try to get along."

"Anyone else want to drive?" asked David, bailing out of his side of the van before anyone could answer.

"I will," said Josh.

"You're only fourteen, Josh," said Doris. "Don't even think about it."

"I'll drive." I pushed Doris off of me and crawled over Josh. Mike moved from the passenger's side and crawled over Josh to my old seat, propping up Doris. David moved to the passenger's side, and Chera, Zach, and Jacob flip-flopped just so they could move a bit.

"Okay, A!" I called out and pointed to the Amoco sign. "Who's playing?"

"I just want a shower," said Doris.

"I can't see now," said Chera.

"My legs hurt too bad," said Josh.

"I'm sound asleep," said David.

Mike was snoring.

I won that game easily. And then I started to get sleepy. "There's a hotel," I called, waking up David somewhere in the middle of Kansas. I pulled in, and David hobbled toward the lobby, his hair sticking up and out at funny angles, his clothes wrinkled like old newspaper. Josh made slow, wobbly laps around the van while we waited. A few minutes later David hobbled back out, shaking his head, and rubbing his eyes. "They're full here. Maybe farther down."

Doris now wanted to drive, only because the driver's seat had the most room. So Mike moved back to the passenger's seat and began to snore there while David and I crawled over Josh and cuddled in the middle seat. Zach, Chera, and Jacob flip-flopped one more time, and now Chera was ready to play the alphabet game.

"What's that funny smell?" asked Zach.

"Oh, my legs," wailed Josh.

Mike snored.

"If you see a rest stop," said David, "I need to go."

"I can't wait to get into that shower." Doris leaned over the steering wheel, straining to see through the bug splotches on the windshield.

"A! Arby's!" Chera shouted, pointing to the big orange sign high above the road. "Is anyone else playing?"

"Hey," I said, "would anyone like to sing choruses?"

I'm pretty sure Michael snorted. But I let it go because I was just happy to be with my family.

We changed drivers four more times before we made it through Kansas, checked twelve more hotels—all full—stopped at five rest stops and three truck stops. Someone at the last hotel in Kansas told us that perhaps across the state line into Missouri we could find something. At sunrise, we arrived at the state line in Kansas City. We stopped at a rest stop overlooking the stadium where the Royals played baseball, and I made everyone pull out toothbrushes and brush their teeth—like a happy family should.

"Well, at least we aren't in Kansas anymore," I said, but everyone else already was asleep. I found myself wondering what that funny smell was.

Missouri was no better. Everywhere we stopped was full. Now no one could drive much more than twenty minutes before pulling over and switching. Once, David got out and tried to lift the van. He said that always gets the blood pumping and wakes you up. He might have lifted it too, but he fell asleep on the hood and I had to go out and wake him up. Once again we crawled over Josh and pulled a double switch with Mike and Doris. In the back, the kids were all propped against each other and sleeping like babies. Every now and then Zach would wake up and ask about that funny smell.

By noon we finally pulled into St. Louis, twenty-four hours after we had left Denver. "They have rooms," Mike said as he walked back to the van. He was nearly weeping. Josh jumped in excitement, but a leg cramp caused him to double over in pain for a few moments. The kids were wide awake and wanted to go to the hotel pool.

"I have to shower," Doris said.

"I'm going to sleep first, or I might drown," said David.

We pulled out the suitcases we needed and walked like zombies to our rooms. Twelve hours, eight showers, sixteen socks, and eight changes of underwear later, we packed back into the minivan and made our way through Illinois and Indiana and on into Ohio.

The next day, when we unloaded the van, I found a plastic bag with its opening tied in a knot. "Phew!" I exclaimed, holding the bag between the thumb and finger of one hand and pinching my nose with the thumb and finger of my other. "What's this?"

David studied it for a moment and then nodded. "Oh, that's Josh's hat."

"Why does it smell so bad?"

"Because Zach threw up in it on the way out there."

"You mean *ten days* ago?"

David nodded. "Just needs to be washed, really, and I think it'll be okay."

Wow! Did I ever get close to my family on that trip. I learned things about them I might never have known had we taken separate cars, or flown, or found a hotel that night in Denver: Doris loves cleanliness; Chera never gets tired of playing the alphabet game; Jacob hates the alphabet game; Josh could never be a contortionist; Mike and David believe if you stick something really smelly into a plastic bag, it'll be okay, even days and days later; and Zach can't eat a candy bar for breakfast before a long road trip.

God knew the desire of my heart. He heard my prayer to draw closer to family. In fact, we got so close there at the end that we all began to smell alike! But God did give us ten wonderful days together in which we laughed and talked and ate and tried to run each other off the road in go-carts.

So many hours all cramped up in a minivan sort of reminded me of another family that spent some time on a big boat for all those days.

They were just lucky they didn't have candy bars back then.

Showtime at the Nursery

Yet when I surveyed all that my hands had done
and what I had toiled to achieve, everything was
meaningless, a chasing after the wind; nothing
was gained under the sun.

ECCLESIASTES 2:11

I just wanted a big, leafy bush to hide the doghouse, that's
all. Our one-hundred-pound dalmatian, SPOT, lives in a little house in the backyard. Weeds grow up around it, and
SPOT has worn a dirt circle out front (mud when it rains).
Whenever I look out my back window, I see this weathered
house in the middle of a small dustbowl (mudbowl when it's
raining), and it hurts my eyes. So I wanted a big, leafy bush
to hide the doghouse.

So David and I drove over to a local nursery looking for
a doghouse-hiding bush. We walked up and down the aisles,

tugging at different tags on the trees and looking at pictures of what the trees were supposed to look like when they grew up. Every so often a sprinkler would turn our way without warning.

"Can I help you?" a man asked in a gruff voice. He was tall and thin, red and weathered from the sun. He had long gray hair that stuck out from beneath a ball cap and a gray, stubbly beard. When he smiled, his face looked as if it hurt him. His lips parted just a bit, and I could see yellowed, crooked teeth. He rubbed the back of his neck with a big, rough hand that made the sound of sandpaper on a board.

"I'm just looking for a bush," I answered.

"Well, let's take a look." He turned and disappeared through the forest that was for sale. I grabbed hold of David's hand and headed after our guide. He led us to a clump of spindly looking bushes with tiny leaves and said, "Here's a real nice crape myrtle." He stroked the branches as if it were a pet. "They grow fast and big and bloom out real pretty in late summer."

I turned the little picture tag so I could see it, and David asked, "Now is this a plant that I would have to spray? Or prune? Or tie up? Or mist? Or—"

"What he wants to know is," I interrupted, "does this plant take a lot of maintenance?"

The man smiled again—pained almost. "Oh, no, just dig a hole and keep it watered."

"Dig a hole?" David asked. "You got anything that just keeps growing in those big buckets they come in?"

"Got some plastic ones inside," the man grumbled.

I elbowed David in the ribs and told the man, "This is nice, but the leaves are so tiny. I'm looking for cover, big cover. I'm looking for something like . . ." I spotted it across the way. "Like that over there!" and I led the way to a thick bush with big, waxy leaves that went all the way to the ground. "Wow, this would hide a car!" I said.

"You want to hide a car?" the man asked.

"Well, no, just a doghouse. And this'll do. I like it."

"You got plenty of shade?" the man asked.

"Not really. The doghouse is out back all by itself. That's why we're looking for a bush."

"Well, this rhododendron bush needs plenty of shade."

"Just what sort of plastic plants do you have inside?" David wanted to know.

The nurseryman ignored David. "I know what you need. Follow me."

Again we were off, zigzagging through lanes of bushes and pots, bags of mulch and manure, and spouting sprinklers until we stopped before a tall, leafy, rather plain-looking plant. The man plucked a couple of dead leaves and rustled the branches a bit, as if to awaken the bush and let it know we were there. I liked the rhododendron better.

"What is it?" I asked.

At first the man stretched out his arms, big and wide, as if he were going to give the bush a hug, but then he let his arms fall to his side. He smiled, and this time it wasn't so much a painful expression but one of true pleasure. He studied the bush, never taking his eyes from it. "*This* is a sweet mock orange."

"I bet you have to water it too, huh?" David asked.

"It looks pretty ordinary," I said. "The leaves are small, the branches are spindly, the height's . . . okay. So why this one? What's so special about it?"

The man from the nursery stepped back from the bush so as not to share the stage with the sweet mock orange. He held up his hands and dramatically indicated the bush before him. "This one," and he nodded and grinned, "this one put on quite a show this spring." That was all he said about the sweet mock orange.

He never told us how to plant it, what sort of soil was best, or if we needed to be cautious of too much sun or too little. To this man, what was important, what was paramount, all that needed to be considered was the *show*.

We stared at the man, who was staring at the bush. Finally, I told David to find a buggy because we were buying the sweet mock orange.

We took the bush home and David dug a hole for it. Then he placed a bench right in front of it. That was back in the summer. When the fall came, so did the frost, and the leaves fell off the bush so that it was bare and far from remarkable. As I'm writing this chapter, spring is drawing near. On warmer days I go out to the garden, sit on the bench, and stare at the bush. I see only a pitiful, leafless thing that could easily be mistaken for dead. But as I sit there, I remember the old man staring at this very same bush and how his grin made even his hardened face pleasant as he thought about "the show."

What I learned from that old man in the nursery (besides which lanes you need to run through really fast or the sprinklers will soak you) is that sometimes the show may not last very long (children grow up, vacations go fast), so you need to enjoy it to the fullest while it's there. Then, when the show is over, you remember it with a fondness and look forward to the next one.

So I sit and stare at the bush, much like Moses must have done when he encountered the burning bush, and wait for the spring, for the blooms the old man said will fill the bush from top to bottom, for the fragrance of oranges, for God to show up and to show off. And I plan to enjoy it!

I may even buy another bush later—one that will hide the doghouse.

Still Trying to Get It through My Thick Head

And I tell you that you are Peter, and on this rock
I will build my church, and the gates of Hades
will not overcome it.

MATTHEW 16:18

As I've traveled around the country, I've been to a lot of churches that just didn't seem like churches. Once, my family and I went to a service in Chattanooga held in a small church that used to be a bar.

"Now this area right here," the pastor told us as we stood where the altar was, "used to be the dance floor."

"Dance floor?" Zach, who was about five at the time, asked.

"That's right." The pastor winked at David and me. "Sometimes, when the Spirit moves just right, a little dancing still goes on right about here."

He led us through the rest of the small building, all painted white and sparkling clean. "These walls were black when we first moved in. And black lights were everywhere. The carpet was so soured it would make you sick. But we ripped it all up, had work days for six Saturdays straight and then prayer one whole day, praying through every single room to bind the demons that once filled the fibers of this place and to cast them all out."

Zachary touched the walls as we passed through, stamped on the used-to-be dance floor, then looked up at the pastor and asked, "What's a black light?"

That night we attended that church. No one danced—even though Zachary was watching for it. But as we sat there, it didn't matter much to us what had gone on in that very spot only a few months earlier. What mattered was that God was there now.

I once spoke at a church in Florida that had once been a computer warehouse—simple concrete floors, exposed steel beams overhead, no pulpit, no baptistry, no nursery, no narthex. Another time I spoke in a barn that had been turned into a church for a group who called themselves Cowboys for Christ. Every Sunday they would tie up their horses outside, stride (some noticeably bowlegged) into the barn, and sit down hat in hand to hear about God, to worship, and to praise. Then after the service, they would ride. That Sunday they even talked me into jumping on a mare and galloping through a dusty field—in my church dress!

But I guess the strangest place I ever spoke was at a saloon in Florida—and it wasn't a building that *used* to be a saloon either. The best I could tell, the church had some sort of a time-share deal going with the saloon's owners. By night the place would be hopping with men and women swaying and staggering to country tunes on the jukebox. But on Sunday mornings the congregation would meet for praise and worship amidst the smells of stale smoke and old beer. One of the ushers would arrive early enough to collect the ashtrays from the tables and to make room for the Bibles and songbooks. Eventually the church raised enough money to shut down the jukebox for good and to hang a sign over the yellowed outline of the words Long Branch Saloon.

I've never thought that church could take place only in a building with a steeple, pews, and a fellowship hall in the back for the potluck dinners. You see, I learned a long time ago, maybe as I watched my own dad, a pastor, hammer and paint and shingle the building of the church he pastored, that the real church is made up of those who come along, bringing their hammers and paintbrushes. The real church is made up of people who visit you when you are ill and who bring you chicken and spaghetti (with no onions because David hates onions), who celebrate the birth of your children with you, who come to see you when you bury a loved one—not even to talk but just to hang out with you and keep you company in case you want to talk. The church is those people who show up for six Saturdays in a row to rip up smelly, moldy carpet and to paint black walls white, those people who push aside ashtrays so they can lay their Bibles flat and follow along in the text with the preacher. That's what I believe, especially after the roof of St. Patrick's Cathedral in New York fell in on me.

I had worked in Newark, New Jersey, the day before, just across from New York City, and David came up to meet me.

Still Trying to Get It through My Thick Head

We thought it would be a blast to spend a summer day in the Big Apple. So we took a cab over the river and told the driver to meet us in front of the cathedral in about five hours, which wasn't nearly enough time for Fifth Avenue alone!

By the time the cab was supposed to pick us up, we were exhausted. "Let's go in," David said, as we stood on the steps of St. Patrick's Cathedral, "just to say we've been there." He always is stepping into doors and then right back out just so he can say he's been there. As a matter of fact, he tried to pull that stunt at Macy's and again at Saks Fifth Avenue, but I wouldn't fall for it.

We walked through the giant opening and into the shady, hushed expanse filled with row after row of pews. Some pews were occupied with people kneeling and leaning forward and praying. Other pews held people aiming video cameras to the front where dim lights glowed and candles flickered, revealing ornate carvings that looked like chairs and gates but were actually church stuff I didn't know the names of or what they were used for. All I know is that everything and everyone seemed very somber.

David and I found a seat in the middle of the cathedral. All alone on the pew, we sat and rested and waited.

I pulled a prayer book from the seat back in front of me and began to thumb through the pages. I could tell David was studying the area up front. "That looks like some sort of big chair up front," he whispered. "Maybe where the head preacher sits."

"Priest, dear. He's called a priest."

"Whatever. It's a big chair."

So there we sat, minding our own business, soaking in the vastness of the building, the awesomeness of the architecture. I was wondering how many of my dad's old churches would fit into this place when something hit me hard on the top of the head, bounced over, hit David in the leg, pinged off the pew, and landed on the hard floor with the sound of a kid's marble bouncing on a sidewalk. I put a hand to my head and rubbed the stinging spot.

David looked up, then hunkered down and grabbed at his leg, sat up, bobbed back down, peered over the edge of the pew to the front and back, and then asked me, "What was that?" He saw me rubbing my head. "Are you all right?"

"Yeah, I think so," I answered. "But that hurt."

Once David gathered his wits, he dove under the pew in front of us and came up with a long piece of gray plaster about the size of a crayon. Then he gazed up, up, up to the ceiling, so arched and gothic. But it was at least fifty feet to the top, so we couldn't tell where the piece had fallen from. I rubbed my head some more. He rubbed his leg. "There's no one in the big chair up front, or I'd tell him about this," he said, waggling the short piece of plaster in the air. "Maybe we'd better get out of here."

So we walked out to wait on the steps. I kept the piece of plaster as a reminder. (I figured the knot on my head would soon go away.) I wanted to remember that no matter how big or famous or impressive the church building, no matter how small or soured, no matter what went on there before, it's just brick, mortar, plaster, and wood (especially if there's one of those big chair things up front).

The real church is the people—the ones who help, the ones who replace all the black light bulbs with bright white ones, the ones who love, the ones who just hang out with you whenever you need someone close. Let this story be a reminder of that truth, and just be glad it didn't take a church roof falling in on you to bring it to mind.

Still Trying to Get It through My Thick Head

chapter
14

Footloose and Fancy Free

Today, if you hear his voice, do not harden your
hearts.

PSALM 95:7B–8A

I have a friend who lost his foot many years ago, although
you wouldn't know it just by looking. He received a prosthesis awhile back and walks without the slightest limp, even
though he's a rather big man.

And of course, he never introduces himself as the guy
with only one foot.

But after you get to know him, if you can catch him late
at night with a group of friends and start swapping stories
and eating hot apple pie, like I did, he'll loosen up and tell

you things—things like the time the doctors discovered a tumor in his right foot and had to operate and eventually take off his foot. And before you can say, "That's terrible!" he'll tell you the story of how he spread the gospel the day his foot fell off in the airport.

"I was racing through the airport one day," said my friend, as he stabbed his hot apple pie with a fork, "pulling one bag behind me and carrying another under my arm, and I was in a big hurry. I was making it along just fine until I came to the escalator. I rode to the bottom, and I guess I just wasn't paying attention, because I didn't step off soon enough and flipped right over my bags and laid out on the floor. I was so embarrassed that I jumped up as quickly as I could."

I gasped and said, "How awful," but he waved me off and continued his story. "A couple of strangers helped me with my bags, and I shot out of there as quickly as I could. To be honest, I think I was more worried about my hair than my foot. As a matter of fact, I never even thought about that." He pointed to his fake foot with his empty fork.

"Anyway, I was heading across the floor again just as fast as I could go but hadn't gotten very far at all when from behind me I heard a woman screaming. I turned around and saw this nicely dressed, respectable-looking woman all red faced and flustered. She was pointing at my foot with one hand and covering her mouth with her other. Her eyes were as big as this saucer." He held up the plate that held his pie. "Without slowing down a bit, I looked at my foot and saw that the prosthesis had twisted all the way around. I was walking as fast as I could with the heel pointed forward and the toe backward."

He chuckled and ate some more pie; some of us were laughing, but most were gasping, just like the woman in the story. I couldn't figure out if I should scream or laugh.

"*Then* tell them what happened," said someone who had heard this story before.

"Well," he continued, and we all held our breath, "I just bent over, grabbed hold of my foot, twisted it around, said, 'Praise the Lord,' and walked on out with my luggage."

Everyone laughed some more. Probably what made us laugh the most was trying to figure out what must have been going on in that poor woman's mind!

It wasn't until much later that I began to think about that story again. (I was on an airplane, and I was laughing, and I'm sure the fellow beside me was a bit worried.) I connected that story with one my pastor told about the shepherds "who had been abiding their flocks in the fields at night."

That night the Good News broke into those shepherds' world with a shattering suddenness. They probably gasped, grabbed at their hearts, maybe even fell down in disbelief at what their ears were hearing and their eyes were seeing. In fact, they were so shaken up that the angels had to assure them everything was going to be all right. "Be not afraid," the angels said.

My preacher even suggested that it's possible not all the shepherds who saw and heard the miracle that night went to search for the babe wrapped in swaddling clothes and lying in a manger. I'd never thought about that before. But I guess when the Good News is announced, we all have the opportunity to accept and embrace it, or reject it and walk away.

Now, I know the sight of a prosthesis spinning around is nothing compared with the glory of angels splitting open the sky and announcing Jesus' birth. But I have thought about how shocked and afraid that woman in the airport must have been when she saw my friend both coming and going at the same time. And when I think about her seeing my friend reach down and twist his foot straight, I'm sure she'll never forget such a sight. (I haven't, and I didn't even see it!) But that same woman, faced with the unbelievable image of my friend, who was once broken but now was walking away, also heard him say, "Well, praise the Lord!"

For just a moment there in the airport, the Good News broke into that woman's world, both in sight and sound. Sometimes encountering God can be downright disturbing, as it must have been for some of the shepherds in the field that night. Sometimes the moment can knock us right off our feet. But what happens in those brief moments afterward can make all the difference—in our lives, sometimes in history. Some of the shepherds went to worship him right away, and some of them probably didn't.

I wonder what the woman in the airport did.

I Once Owned a Chevette

Train a child in the way he should go, and when
he is old he will not turn from it.

PROVERBS 22:6

I once tried to run away from God in a Chevette. Actually,
I was headed to my mother's house, which was probably not
the place to go if I was trying to get away from God. I knew
Mom would ask me all the tough questions: "Are you going
to church on Sundays?" "Are you reading your Bible?"
"Quote me a Scripture verse—don't think, just quote one."

I had been away at college for a few months—not long
enough to find the answers I was looking for. I had so many
questions about God, and all of them began with why. Why

did my big sister have to be killed in a car accident? Why did my little sister have to die of leukemia? Why did my father have to divorce my mother? *How many years of college would it take to figure out stuff like that?* I wondered.

But Mom had called and wanted me to come home for the weekend. I didn't want to go if all she talked about was how good God had been to her. I told myself that if I got the old "God's ways are not our ways" lecture again, I would just turn my little Chevette around and go back to my dorm.

I bought my Chevette brand-new in 1980 at 19 percent interest and thought that was pretty good. I especially liked the new plastic smell that reminded me of the blow-up toys you can buy for the swimming pool. The car was silver with a red interior. The sad thing about my Chevette is that it began to fall apart not long after I bought it.

The tires wore unevenly, and the car began to shake. Soon one headlight burned out and the right turn signal stopped working. Some people laughed when the driver's-side door fell off. I was so embarrassed to have to stop the car, get out in the middle of traffic, pick up my door, and slide it in the hatchback.

Later (and long before he was my husband) I met David, and he tried to help by tying on the door with a coat hanger. It helped some, but now I couldn't open the door at all. And shortly after that the passenger's-side window fell down into the door panel. David had to take off the panel and wiggle the glass back on the track, but anytime someone even touched it, it would disappear into the door.

I was still going to see Momma, no matter that the gearshift knob had come off right there in my hand one day, nearly causing me to wreck. Not even duct tape could fix that, so I just stuck a potato on the gear stick. Neither did the car have air conditioning, and now that one window was broken and the other door was wired shut, all I could do was leave the hatchback open, drive fast, and stay away from bumps in the road that would cause the back lid to slap closed. But I was still going to see Momma.

At least I had a radio. From the very beginning I had a radio. I thought it was well worth the extra monthly payment because it was a nice, push-button, lighted-faced AM radio. At any given time I had access to five talk shows, eight country music stations, three gardening shows, and one farm report. At least Merle Haggard could drown out the rattles.

On the day I tried to outrun God, things had just added up way too much. I wasn't happy with how life had turned out, how loved ones had died even though they had loved God so much, about how hard it was to work full-time and go to school full-time, about how my car was falling apart and I couldn't seem to do anything about it (the potato on the stick shift was only temporary).

This wasn't the first time I had been angry with God, just the first time I happened to be in my Chevette when the anger hit. I stamped the gas and set a course down the interstate. The wind was blowing in through half a dozen different holes and cracks, so I reached to turn on the radio, hoping Merle Haggard or Conway Twitty or even that guy who told me how much cows were selling for would drown out the roar and the rattle. But the knob came off in my hand, *and the radio died!* I punched all the buttons over and over and banged on the dash and heard a new rattle, but no music.

Why did God let *that* happen? I was on the edge, and all I really needed was one good country music station and I would be just fine, but God took even that away.

I would not be defeated. *I'll sing*, I thought. *I can sing loud enough to drown out all these noises.* So I began to hum and then to sing. I was on the second verse of a song before I realized I was singing "Victory in Jesus."

Oh, no, God, you're not going to get me that easy, I thought. *I was angry with you before, and now my radio's broken, so you think I'm going to sing church songs?*

I searched my memory and began to sing some old Beatles song. "We all live in a yellow submarine! A yellow submarine! A yellow submarine! And we're a part of the family—the family of God."

Two or three more times I tried to sing Merle or Conway, but every time, I would end up sliding into a Southern Gospel camp meeting song that praised the Lord. In the midst of my Chevette storm there on I-40, going at least fifty-five and hanging on to the wheel with both hands, I began to sing, "Amazing grace, how sweet the sound." Tears began to flow (and the wind blew them across my face), but I kept on singing the songs of my childhood, the songs that made sinners weep and saints dance. Even when I shifted into fifth gear and the potato came off in my hand again, I was singing "How Great Thou Art."

God, indeed, inhabits the praises of his people, even if one of his people is rattling down the highway in a silver Chevette with one door wired shut, the hatchback flapping, and no radio. I exited the highway and drove to my mom's house and gave her a big hug. She could tell I'd been crying.

"Oh, darling, did something else on that car break today?" she asked.

I nodded.

"Well, I can't fix your car, but just do what I do when bad things keep piling up like that."

"What's that, Mom?"

"Just start singing hymns, one after the other," she said. "I know you remember them. If you'll just do that, God will fill up all the hurting places, and you'll feel better in no time."

I wondered if Mom had ever owned a Chevette. But then again, I remembered she had had her own hurting places—much worse than a rattling car.

She was right. Praises—not an AM radio—calm the storm, quiet the noises, and still the quaking heart. When I finally sold the car, lots more wire and tape held it together inside and out than that day I tried to outrun God. A hole in the floorboard was getting bigger every day, and the potatoes never lasted very long. I sold the Chevette for three hundred dollars at zero interest to someone who didn't mind crawling in through the hatchback, which I thought was a pretty good deal for a ten-year-old Chevette—and an even better deal for a silver cathedral with a red interior.

You'll Never Have to Dust Again

> Teach them [God's words] to your children, talking about them when you sit at home and when you walk along the road, when you lie down and when you get up.
>
> DEUTERONOMY 11:19

I don't know why I said yes to the fellow, maybe because never having to dust again sounded so ... romantic!

"You mean, not even a little?" I asked him on the telephone.

"If you get this thing set up right," he answered, "use it frequently—like every day—then you can take all your old dust rags and throw them away. And then there are the health benefits for your children."

"For the children?"

"Yes, ma'am. Helps them to breathe easier."

"Really?" Anything to help my children breathe easier must be a good thing.

"Oh yeah."

"Well, then," I said, "I guess we need to talk."

"How about tomorrow night?" he asked. "I'll have someone in your neighborhood who will be glad to demonstrate our machine for you."

That sounded perfect, and so the next night I warned David, before he had a chance to take off his work boots and walk around in his stained socks or loosen his belt or something like that, that we had company coming.

"So what kind of machine is it?" David asked, lacing his boots back up.

"I'm not sure," I answered. "He didn't give a lot of information over the phone."

"Sort of like a snowplow, you think?"

I frowned at David and told him to tuck in his shirttail.

Soon a man showed up at the front door carrying a big, black notebook under one arm and dragging R2-D2 at his side.

"Come right in," I said.

"My name's Chuck." He let go of the little robot to shake our hands. We led him into the living room, and he wheeled his contraption right along with him. "So you hate to dust?"

"It's no big deal, really," David said.

"Hate it with a passion," I interjected.

"Then you're going to love this." Chuck took a seat on our sofa and plopped the big notebook down on the coffee table in front of him. "Oh, would it be possible to get a drink of water?"

I left and returned with a glass of water to find Chuck and David bent over the robot, examining and punching buttons.

"It's a vacuum cleaner!" David said, looking up and smiling. "Chuck says this thing will pick up a bowling ball!"

"Why would you want to pick up a bowling ball?" I asked.

"If it can pick up a bowling ball," explained Chuck, "imagine what it can do with a speck of dust."

David whistled at the overwhelming notion.

"Here's your water," I said, handing over the glass. "Now tell me about the no dusting part again."

Chuck took the glass and turned it upside down so that water and ice plopped right there on the carpet in the middle of the living room floor. "Oops," he said, but he didn't seem too upset about his mess. "Good thing I've got the model 500, series A, with me." He plugged his contraption into the wall, pulled out a coiled hose, telescoped out a silver wand, flipped on a toggle switch, and with a whine and a blare, the squatty little machine came to life. Chuck aimed the nozzle at the puddle on the carpet. The ice rattled as it was sucked up the silver wand, and in two seconds the spot was clean and nearly dry.

"Wow!" David said, as the whine of the machine died down.

"Kind of loud, isn't it?" I said.

"I bet you can pick up nuts and bolts with that thing," said David.

Chuck nodded.

"And wood chips!"

Chuck nodded again.

"And—"

"What about the dust?" I interrupted before we wound up back at the bowling ball. "And the easier breathing for the children?"

Chuck's face brightened. "Ah yes, the dust and the breathing. Let me explain that, but first, let me show you some pictures." He turned the black notebook so David and I could see it easily and then began to flip through some laminated pages. He turned until he came to a big color photo of a space alien, with giant, toothy chompers and long, hairy legs, and an antlike body with big, bulging eyeballs. I pulled back in disgust.

"Scary, isn't it?" Chuck's voice was flat and emotionless, like those characters whose brains were sucked out by the pod people in that old black-and-white movie *Invasion of the Body Snatchers*.

My hand was over my mouth, and I was afraid I wouldn't be able to speak, so I just nodded.

"Caught a big bass once on something that looked like that." David leaned in to get a good look at the picture.

"This," began Chuck, tapping the alien in his notebook, "is a dust mite. The picture's been blown up about a hundred times because the real mite is only the size of a dust speck." Chuck paused to allow us to soak in the dust-sized alien.

"Ma'am, how many children do you have?" he asked me.

I found my voice and eked out a weak, "Two."

Chuck dropped his head, rubbed the back of his neck, moved his hand up to his forehead, rubbed his eyes, and finally finished at his chin before saying in a most somber voice, "Then you need to hear this."

"Hear what?" David said.

I Can See Myself in His Eyeballs

"That these dust mites," he thumped the big, glossy photo on the table, "could be everywhere in this house. In your carpet, on your sofa." He slapped the couch. "On these pillows." He squeezed one of my throw pillows and then threw it to the far end of the couch. "On your curtains, and . . ." Now he closed his eyes as if the dread of what he was about to say was more than he could bear, "Even in the beds where your children sleep—heaven forbid."

"Wait one minute!" David nearly shouted. "If this thing here," and he slapped the robot vacuum, "can pick up a bowling ball, it can surely suck up a freaky looking, itsy-bitsy dust mite!"

Chuck smiled smugly and nodded.

"How can we get rid of them?" I asked.

"How can we zap 'em?" David slapped a fist into an open palm.

Chuck walked over to his machine and unfastened the hose. "Just leave this off, pour water into this opening until it's full, and press the start button." He pressed the button again, and the thing whirred to life for the second time that evening. For a couple of minutes, a thunderous roar filled the room. He finally punched it off. "If you do that on a regular basis, no more dust, no more dust mites. And your children can breathe easier and rest peacefully."

"Not while it's running." David massaged his eardrums.

"And how long should I let the thing run?" I asked.

"About an hour," he said.

An hour!? "And how often?"

"Every day."

"Just don't leave any bowling balls out, right?" David said, but Chuck ignored him.

"And how much does something like this cost?" David asked.

Chuck pointed at the picture of the dust mite on my coffee table and said, "To rid your home and your children's beds of these . . . ungodly creatures . . . sixteen hundred dollars."

David's eyes grew as large as the dust mites' enlarged one hundred times. "We didn't pay that much for our car."

"We have financing available," Chuck informed us.

David looked at me. I was wearing my death-to-the-dust-mite expression.

"This thing will have to suck up an awful lot of dust mites," he said. He thought a little longer and then asked Chuck, "What's the *worst* these creatures can do to the children?"

I punched David in the arm and asked Chuck to please explain to us about the financing.

"A good snowplow costs you about six hundred bucks," David grumbled. I punched him in the arm again.

Chuck broke all the numbers down for us. He even told us how many dust mites could fit onto the head of a pin and explained that with one push of a button, we could wipe out thousands, maybe even millions, of the little buggers. When it became clear to David how we actually were paying less than a penny per mite, the deal wasn't such a bad one after all.

And me? Well, I wheeled that little robot man all over the house and sucked up pillows and curtains and Lego's and little green army men—and got real close to the cat once. For a while, I would turn on the machine every day and leave it in the middle of the room to roar and whine for at least an hour, sucking up the evil dust mites. So what if we were all slowly losing our hearing? *It will be worth it*, I thought. *After all, isn't cleanliness next to godliness?*

Twelve years later, we still have that old machine—and it's paid for now. (Whenever I need a credit reference, I list my vacuum cleaner finance company.) I don't know how many dust mites we conquered with it over the years. Probably not many, because the thing was too stinking loud to live with. Sometimes David would hop about on the carpet and then announce to me that he had squashed enough for today, just so I wouldn't turn on the machine. Other times he and the children would hop around and have big dust mite-squashing parties. I would always make refreshments.

Sometimes our good intentions can drown out what's really important to a family. David and I wanted so badly to wage war against all the dust mites of the world. But what God reminded me of—and in the roar of a vacuum cleaner, no less—is that there are more important things we can do for our children, like teach them the truths of God. And that's hard to do with something as loud as a 747 roaring in the living room every day.

Our battle against dust mites goes on. Today, when we sit down on the sofa for family time, we like to think we squashed a few for the cause. But what we have to pass on to our children doesn't have anything to do with a vacuum cleaner.

So if you're interested in a vacuum that can pick up bowling balls, we'll have it in our next yard sale—financing available.

Truck-Stop Rose

Don't be deceived, my dear brothers. Every
good and perfect gift is from above, coming
down from the Father of the heavenly lights, who
does not change like shifting shadows.

JAMES 1:16–17

Before my husband and I were married, I don't think anyone ever told him he was supposed to buy me an anniversary
gift *every* year. But through seventeen years of marriage,
that's just one of those things he's had to learn. Thank goodness we've always lived close to a 7-11 (or a truck stop), and
they sell those funny cards close to the cash register. You
know, the ones that read, "Happy anniversary to the one I
love, and welcome to Tennessee!"

I've received a few of those over the years, along with
some nail clippers that have a catcher on the side for the

trimmings, sort of like a lawnmower; some collector spoons of the states of Alabama and Arkansas; and a whole case of 10W-40 motor oil.

But the greatest gift came the year I received a dusty rose that really wasn't a rose at all.

Since our anniversary is in May, every now and then it falls close to Mother's Day. One year it fell on Mother's Day, and I knew right then I was going to get gypped—I always do on those two-for-one holidays. As we scrambled to pull ourselves and the children together for church, my husband suddenly froze up, turned white, and said, "Why don't you and the children head on to church, and I'll meet you there."

"Need to make a stop?" I knew right away what had happened—or in this case, had not happened.

He nodded, but not a big nod, somehow believing he would give away the "surprise" with a big nod.

The children and I headed on to church, stopping for doughnuts along the way, which gave David enough time to do his shopping and still arrive before me. He was standing in the foyer when we walked in, and beaming, obviously holding something behind his back.

"Hi, honey." His face was about to break into a giant smile. Then he quickly pulled from behind him a silky—dusty—gray rose. "Happy anniversary *and* happy Mother's Day," he said. (Told you.)

I took the rose from him and thanked him while studying the flower. Something looked odd here, something besides the dust.

"It's a rose," he said.

"Yes."

"For Mother's Day."

"Yes."

"*And* our anniversary."

(Gypped.) "Yes."

Once I brushed away some of the dust, the flower didn't look nearly as gray. It looked almost white. I could even see the detail in the lace that edged some of the petals. One of the petals was more crooked than the others, so I gave it a little tug, and just like that the whole rose sprung open and dangled there before me like a broken Slinky. It took me only a couple of seconds before I realized that the rose wasn't a rose at all—it was underwear! And I'm not talking about the Fruit of the Loom kind either. This was more like dental floss! My mouth dropped open, David turned whiter than the rose—I mean, underwear—and Zach, who was six then, called out, "Go, Dad!" right there in the church foyer!

I hid the . . . the . . . *thing* behind my back just as some of our church friends walked by.

"Good morning, Margaret," I said, waving with my Bible.

"Good morning, Chonda," said Margaret. "My, you look like you got some sun this weekend."

Now I was fanning myself with my Bible. "Oh, yeah, I'm feeling just a little flushed."

I shoved stem and all into my purse, and somehow we shuffled on into the sanctuary. I think David and I were content to put this little incident behind us. Then the preacher called the ushers forward and announced to the congregation that because it was Mother's Day, he wanted to make sure every mother there received her special flower.

Uh-oh.

Truck-Stop Rose

The ushers had baskets filled with red and white carnations, and the men moved along the aisles, passing out the fresh flowers. David took a single carnation from the basket and handed it to me, just as he had with the fake flower earlier. Everything seemed to be okay. It looked as if we were going to get out of this whole mess without any major embarrassment. That is, until Zach called from the far end of the row, "Hey, Dad, do you think that one will turn into underwear too?"

I learned that day that looks can be so deceiving. I know that's one of those real simple lessons you learn when you're two and the pretty bumblebee makes you cry. But sometimes those simple lessons need to be reviewed. I don't think there's any better way to be reminded than by unwrapping a pair of underwear in the church foyer. Yup, appearances can be very deceiving.

Papaw's Shiny Red Truck

For he will command his angels concerning you
to guard you in all your ways.

PSALM 91:11

Not long ago my husband and I took a trip to the Holy
Land with our church family. Sixteen of us motored up from
Galilee into the Golan Heights area and the northern edge
of the small country of Israel. We witnessed the remnants of
a recent and deadly war: burned-out buildings riddled with
bullet holes; tank and truck carcasses, some upright and half-
buried by the landscape, others flipped over and half-buried
by the landscape.

"Now that fence straight ahead—the one with the
barbed wire across the top—is the Syrian border." Our guide

pointed through the bus's front glass. Most of us just nodded, some raised their eyebrows, others said things like, "Ah." We drove a bit farther, parallel with the winding, barbed fence a few miles, when the guide pointed again and said, "Now we are driving along the Lebanese border." More nods, more raised eyebrows, more ahs. Then we looped around and headed south, following the Jordanian border and more barbed wire fence all the way to the Dead Sea.

We changed into our swimsuits and dove into the salty water—and floated. We couldn't go under if we tried. A dozen of us bobbed around like corks, arms splashing, toes sticking straight up. David covered himself in the mineral-rich mud and jumped around and hooted like a mud monster would do—just being silly in a foreign country.

A couple of days later as we sat in a hotel room in Jerusalem, we saw on the news that a missile had been fired by a Lebanese battalion and had exploded on a highway just across the border in Israel. David sat up on the edge of the bed (from time to time I was still finding bits of that mud in his ears, his hair, etc.), pointed at the television, and said, "We were just there! I can't believe this. Did our guide say anything about our being in a danger zone? No, she just pointed and said, 'By the way, Lebanon is right over there—on the other side of that fence.' Not one word about *watch out for the missiles!*"

Once David calmed down (and I made him scrub behind his ears and the back of his neck real good this time), we thanked God for the protection of his big old arms.

Not very long after that, God wrapped those same protective arms around Chera. Instead of ending tragically, it was a night she merely managed to scare a few cattle.

David and I had traveled to Dallas and had left the grand-parents in charge of Chera and Zach, which we did from time to time. Only now, Chera had her driver's permit.

We had just gone to bed when the phone rang, and I grabbed it up halfway through the first ring. (The phone never rings that late when I'm on the road.)

"Hello?" I said.

"Mom?"

"Yes, Chera. What's wrong?" My heart was pounding. David rose up on his elbows and listened.

"Just wanted to let you know I had a little accident," she said, "but everything's *fine* now."

"What kind of an accident?"

Her voice sounded fine, but my heart was pounding so hard I put a hand on my chest to quiet it.

"Really, it's okay. They were letting me drive, and I went off the road a little bit."

"A little bit?"

Then Nanny took the phone. "I'm sorry to bother you. She's *fine*, and everyone is *fine*, and we're taking care of everything. She just wanted you to know. But don't worry. Everything is *fine*."

"You're sure?"

"I'm sure. It's just *fine*."

I hung up, and David said, "Is everything all right? What kind of an accident?"

"I guess Chera ran Nanny's car off the side of the road, but Mom says everything is fine, just fine." Then we went to sleep.

Not until we got home the next day were we able to wash away the mud from this scene and begin to see exactly what

Papaw's Shiny Red Truck

had taken place and just how much God must have watched over our little girl.

"Come here, Chera," I said, giving my daughter a big hug. "I guess Nanny was a bit rattled when you wound up on the shoulder of the road."

"Not really," Chera answered. I raised my eyebrows. "She wasn't there," she explained. "Just Papaw."

"You and Papaw were driving Nanny's car?"

"No. We were driving Papaw's truck."

"Papaw's truck? You mean the little red truck with the chrome trim and the roll bar and the toolbox and the fog lights and the mudflaps with the little reflectors on them and a shine that always looks like it just rolled off the showroom floor? *That* truck?"

Chera nodded.

"Did it mess anything up?" I asked. I was worried about the mudflaps.

"It was hard to tell. The wrecker driver said—"

"Wrecker? You had to call a wrecker?"

"Just one. And he was really nice. He even went to the hardware store and bought some more wire."

"Wire for what?"

"For the fence."

"What fence?"

"The one I landed on afterward."

"After what?"

"After I hit the mailbox."

"You hit a mailbox?"

Chera grimaced. "Two of them."

We drove out to see where Chera had plowed through a couple of mailboxes and landed on top of a fence. Papaw already had put up two new cedar posts and replaced the mailboxes. The new barbed wire shone like I remembered Papaw's truck shining. Two long, deep tire ruts trailed from the edge of the asphalt and ended just on the other side of the fence. Some of the brush and small trees had been pulled up, torn and snapped off by Papaw's shiny bumper. Not far away was a telephone pole, solid and hard. Not far away was a ditch, deep and steep. Not far away cars zoomed past, fast and close. I grabbed Chera and held her and told her never, ever to wreck like that again. She said she wouldn't.

As we drove away, Chera pointed to some big, brown cows meandering through the field. "There must have been fifty of them standing around Papaw's truck that night." She smiled as she remembered this. "Just standing and looking at us, not scared at all."

Chera probably will remember the cows, I thought. But not until she's older, maybe not even until she's had children of her own, will she recall how God put his big, old arms around her, or will she remember the angels—the ones who surely must have hovered right there that night, beside the cows and around Papaw's shiny red truck. Then she'll see more clearly.

chapter
19

Salvation in the Driveway

The LORD does not look at the things man looks at.
Man looks at the outward appearance, but the
LORD looks at the heart.

1 SAMUEL 16:7b

When I was just a kid, I named this woman at church Sister Seatsaver. I called her that because every Sunday she arrived early to lay a scarf on the seat next to her, to save that seat for her cousin. Then one day I noticed she plopped down her purse in the seat next to the seat covered with her scarf—for her aunt. Then another Sunday I noticed she laid out her scarf, her purse, and a pair of gloves so the fourth pew looked like a ladies department store. If she brought any more family with her, she was going to have to go to Sunday school naked!

Sometimes I couldn't help myself. While everyone else was in Sunday school, I grabbed her stuff and spread it around on other pews—just to see if she was saved.

It's funny what you can figure out about people by watching them when they don't think anyone else is looking. I'm not talking about spying; I'm just talking about eye-balling the situation, paying attention to how someone behaves when the scarf has been moved, or as was the case with my husband, when an old bus and a trailer got stuck in our driveway.

Most of the time when I travel, I take a big bus with a kitchen and a bathroom. We move a lot slower than an air-plane, of course, but we have better snacks. The un-nice part of the deal is that the bus will show up at my house at mid-night to pick up all my stuff and me. David usually sits up with me and helps me carry on my hang-up clothes, even though he can hardly keep his eyes open. Most of the time I'm all loaded in fifteen minutes, and David can go to sleep. But this one night was a different story.

It was past midnight, rainy and cool, and the bus still hadn't shown up. David was sitting on the end of the couch, nodding off.

"Here's the bus!" I called when I heard the rumble com-ing down the street.

David jumped up and wiped the drool from the corner of his mouth. "I'm awake! I'm awake!"

In the drizzle we loaded my suitcases on the bus while the driver hooked up the trailer that had been parked in our driveway. When he was finished, we were finished, and he pulled forward while David waited in his Jeep in the street so he could pull back in after we left. But the bus or trailer—or both—made the most awful scraping sound I'd ever heard. From the back of the bus I looked out the window. I couldn't see much of anything except the neighbor's lights coming on.

I watched David hop out of his Jeep and, in the glow of the red bus lights, motion for the driver to back up. The reverse lights shone brightly in David's face now, and he didn't seem too happy.

The driver revved the engine, and the wheels whined on the wet pavement. Smoke puffed up in front of David. He was standing with his hands on his hips staring at the back of the bus, as if he were memorizing the 1-800 number he was supposed to call to say what he thought about this driver's skills.

I noticed that the lights from the neighbor on the other side of our house and two from across the street were on. I decided to stay in the bus.

The driver had climbed out and was talking to David. From what I could tell by David's and the driver's body language, the driver was going to try it again. David made a small bus with one hand and used the palm of his other for a driveway. He showed the driver how he wanted him to back up all the way to his elbow, get a running start, and leap over the little dip where the street and the drive met. (I hoped *leap* wasn't the word he used.)

So the driver hopped back in the bus, backed it up, and SCREEEECH! went the trailer against the concrete. I was just waiting for the neighbors to start shooting. The trailer tongue was plowing into the driveway as if it were planting season.

Together the bus driver and David wrestled with some connections, and the trailer broke loose and dropped to the

Salvation in the Driveway

driveway with a bang. Now the bus moved forward, and David backed up his Jeep (his pretty, red Jeep) to the trailer and, with some finagling that I couldn't totally see from where I was, hooked it up, causing his Jeep to stand almost straight up. I could see the top of his head peeping up over the dash and wanted to laugh—but didn't.

With more scraping and screeching, he dragged the trailer from the drive to the middle of the street and unhooked it. Then the bus driver tried to match up the bus to the trailer in the dark, in the rain. He would pull up, then back, then up, then back. Every time he revved the engine, I'd hide my head under a pillow and pray the neighbors weren't calling the police. Whenever I'd peep up and look out, I'd see David standing there soaked, and when he would wave the bus back, one arm swishing and the other held up high, he looked like a set of broken wiper blades.

David and the driver then worked to rehook the hitch. But apparently whatever they were doing wasn't working. David disappeared into the garage.

He reappeared with a big claw hammer in one hand and slowly slipped up behind the driver and—for just a moment—I gasped. Then I watched David use the hammer to pound on the trailer hitch. PING, PING, PING! Maybe the neighbors hadn't noticed ...

Finally, the hitch must have matched up with the trailer because I saw David throw up his arms, much like a referee signaling a touchdown. He brushed off his hands, shook with the bus driver, then went over and leaned against his Jeep, hammer in hand, and watched us pull away.

It was well after one o'clock in the morning by now, and there, beneath the street lamp, with the trailer out of the way,

I could better see the groove in the middle of the driveway. The light rain had filled it up with water, and it looked like a miniature river—the kind at the bottom of the Grand Canyon.

I waited long enough to give David time to get inside and change into some dry clothes before I called him.

"Hello?" He already sounded sleepy.

"Hi, honey. Looks like you guys had a rough time out there," I said, cautious about how I approached this.

"Wow," he said, "I didn't think we were ever going to get that thing out of there."

"Did it tear up a lot—you know—of the driveway?" I asked.

"Got a big trough right in the middle," he said, "but I think I can fix it."

"Is your Jeep okay?"

"Can't hurt the Jeep," he answered.

"Back okay? Toes okay?"

"Everything's fine, praise the Lord!"

The way I see it, if you can wrestle with a trailer in the rain at one o'clock in the morning, do enough damage to your driveway to make Bob Vila cry, and still praise the Lord, then I guess you're saved. Praise the Lord!

chapter 20

Twins?!

And we know that in all things God works for the
good of those who love him, who have been
called according to his purpose.

ROMANS 8:28

I'll never forget the look on David's face the day the twins
came home.

"Twins?" asked David, standing at the door in his dirty
work clothes. "How did this happen?"

I was standing by the two baby carriers, wringing my
hands because I had been afraid he would ask that. "Come,
look at these precious babies." I pushed aside just enough of
the blankets to show their faces. "Oh, look," I almost sang,
staring into the little dark faces of the six-week-old girls.

David moved close enough so he could see them, and that was good. "Wow, they sure are small. And there are *two* of them."

"That's why they're called twins, honey," I said.

Then he shook his head, as if snapping out of a trance. "Twins? How did that happen?"

The beautiful, biracial babies had been abandoned for more than twenty-four hours and needed emergency placement until more permanent arrangements could be made. David and I were still kids ourselves, not much more than twenty, but we had volunteered to be foster parents. The state would pay for all the diapers and formula.

"How much trouble could a little baby be, anyway?" we had asked ourselves when we first had signed up for this venture. After all, Chera was a year old, and things had gone pretty smoothly with her.

"We have twins," I told David, "because that's the way this one comes."

"But we don't know anything about taking care of twins." David instinctively rocked one carrier and then the other.

"Okay, then, so you take care of one, and I'll get the other," I told him.

"It's just . . ." Now he was staring at the tiny faces. "It's just that now it's not a matter of simple addition."

"What do you mean?"

"Now it's a matter of multiplication. Everything—food, diapers, burping, teething—is multiplied by two! And . . ."

"And what?"

"What if you get attached to them like you did with Joseph?"

That hit me hard. Joseph was a baby boy we had taken in for four months before his adoptive parents could take him home. I got to meet them and to place the child I'd grown so accustomed to into that new mother's arms. She was blubbering because she was getting a new baby boy, and I was blubbering because I was giving up my new baby boy.

"That's just the chance I'll have to take," I said. "Just like we did with Tracy."

David frowned, remembering six-year-old Tracy, who had lived with us for two weeks and whose schoolteacher called us in one day and asked us not to feed him anything with sugar in it before school. (What his teacher didn't know was that he bounced off the walls in the evening as well, all the way up to bedtime.) His mom was in drug rehab, and his dad was in jail. We found out he could sing like a songbird. The day he left us he called David Daddy.

"And don't forget Andrew," added David. Andrew was an African-American baby who, at three months old, was bigger than Chera, who was nearly a year old. David wanted to keep him. "He's going to grow up to play football one day, and we could have free tickets!" But after about a month, Andrew went to a new home too.

Taking care of the twins turned out to be like David had said: We multiplied everything by two. Feed twice, change twice, burp twice, and . . . and what was that rash? We bundled up the twins and Chera, packed everyone into the Chevette, and drove straight to the doctor, who laid the tiny ones out on his examining table. They were all spotted now and wailing in stereo.

"Yep," said the doctor. "Just what I thought. Sort of unusual at this age."

"What?" David and I said together, as if *we* were twins.

Twins?!

"Chicken pox."

"Chicken pox?" we repeated.

"Yep," he said, looking into their ears. "And it's a safe bet that your other little one there will have them in a few weeks. Looks like you've got *three* of them to work through now."

Three? The math was getting worse!

The doctor gave us some pink lotion, and every day and night we coated the little girls in pink and rocked them until they stopped crying. We didn't get much sleep that week. Once the worst of the red spots cleared up, we received a call. The twins were going home.

Only an hour after they left, David took me to the emergency room, where the doctor checked me in. I was exhausted to the point of passing out. But I stayed only twenty-four hours and was back in plenty of time to rub our own baby daughter down in pink lotion and to rock her to sleep too.

I wondered for a long time about the year we were foster parents. What good did we do? The children were with us only for a little while. It's not like we had lots of time to teach them things like respect, hard work, or how to make pancakes, or to fish, or to whistle. We were just a layover, a weigh station, a rest stop. We fed them, bathed them, loved them, sang over them, prayed over them, and then we passed them on so they could get on with the rest of their lives.

That's what I used to think until recently, after a concert in middle Tennessee. A man and a woman with a son about the age of my daughter approached me. The mother said, "You may not remember me, but I remember you. You were the one who carried my baby to me about twelve years ago and placed him in my arms."

My heart nearly stopped as I thought about the day I handed over baby Joseph.

"And this is our son," she added, her hands on the shoulders of a fine-looking young man. He had golden hair and a big smile that had lost all of its baby fat.

"Joseph?" I asked.

"We named him Shane," the mother said.

I gave him a big hug and remembered that the last time I had touched him, I was holding him in my arms too.

"My, how you've grown," I said, sounding so silly.

Shane didn't say much. He just shoved his hands into his pockets and grinned. (I never remembered him being that quiet.)

"I wanted to thank you," said the mother, "for all you did for Shane." She daubed at her tears with the back of her hand. The father was grinning and trying not to cry. "We saw your picture in the paper, and I knew that was you."

"Shoot," I said, trying not to cry as well, "all I did was feed him and change his diaper." Shane blushed. But I knew what she meant, and I thanked her for saying so.

Sometimes we may not know what God is doing in our lives. And if we do know what, we may not know why. Then sometimes, God opens up a small window that allows us to look back over a portion of our lives, and in a small way, we understand the connection. I thanked him for the simple glimpse that night.

Maybe one day I'll hear that Tracy is singing in a band somewhere, that the twins are supermodels and famous, and that Andrew is playing for the Packers and has free tickets with our names on them. But even if that never happens, David and I know we loved our houseful of kids, and God used that year for his own purposes in each person's life— those who passed through quickly and those of us who lingered together longer.

Noisy Mimes in Indianapolis

The trumpeters and singers joined in unison, as with one voice, to give praise and thanks to the LORD. Accompanied by trumpets, cymbals and other instruments, they raised their voices in praise to the LORD and sang: "He is good; his love endures forever."

2 CHRONICLES 5:13

The mimes were so noisy that weekend—well, not the mimes really but those around them. We were at Bill and Gloria Gaither's Praise Gathering in Indianapolis, and right there, in the middle of the hallway, these mime artists were walking around like robots—bending, stepping, waving as if they had rusty joints. Ten-year-old Zachary stepped into the middle of them and did his own tin man strut. The crowd that had gathered loved it and roared with laughter, and that made Zach blush. That was a pretty loud scene.

But maybe the loudest part of the whole weekend was Saturday night after the service when we took my mom; my stepdad, Sammy; and some of their friends to a sit-down supper at a local restaurant. That night Mom shared one story after another and had her friends and waiters alike laughing and slapping one another and dropping dishes on the floor. That was a loud moment.

David thought the five-hour drive from Nashville was one of the loudest weekend moments. I had flown into Indianapolis, but he had driven up with my mom and my Aunt Ruth. He said every mile had a story to go with it, some stories going way back to 1913. David said it was like listening to two books on tape at once.

The whole weekend was just designed to be loud. Twelve thousand people sang and laughed together and then milled about in hallways too small for that many folks. Old friends saw one another across the sea of people and yelled real loud because it was so noisy. Then they pushed through the crowd for a hug and even more yells. Some of the artists in the booths that lined the hallways played videos and CDs and cranked the volume up loud enough so it could be heard above the people who were yelling because they hadn't seen each other in a dozen years.

Sometimes I would step outside just to listen to the soothing sounds of traffic—and the man on the street corner. A black man with an armful of papers, waving them about his head and shouting about God's love. All weekend he was there—early in the morning as we headed out and searched for breakfast and then again that evening as we headed back to the hotel for bed. He was always there, waving the papers and proclaiming God as King.

I Can See Myself in His Eyeballs

I bought one of the man's papers and thanked him for what he was doing. He said, "Praise God!" in a big, booming voice and returned to proclaiming the same Good News to the world (or at least to Indianapolis).

Some people thought the Katinas were the loud part. They were a group of young men from Samoa, and they had drums and guitars. When they played, the floor shook, and some people put their hands over their ears. Other people stood and clapped and danced about and made the floor shake even more. The Katinas sang about a great Redeemer that we serve—a mighty, awesome God. And they sang it loudly!

Some may have thought the banjo player was the loudest thing there—especially those who don't like the banjo, like my mom. Or maybe the loudest moment was when T. D. Jakes belted out a sweaty message, a message that rolled out into the hallway and caused people stopping at the water fountain to stroll over and take a peek inside.

All weekend long the Good News of God rang out in Indianapolis, from the street corners, from the hallways, from the stages. But the thing that stopped me that weekend, that caused me to listen, that caused me to weep, was not the noise, the shouting, the booming, or the volume. No, silence—and the words that came out of it—halted me.

Only a few days before this Praise Gathering, professional golfer Payne Stewart died in a bizarre plane crash. Something had gone wrong with his private plane, and the jet traveled for more than seven hours on autopilot from Florida to South Dakota, where it finally crashed in an open field.

Noisy Mimes in Indianapolis

Payne was a great golfer and a great Christian, so when the memorial service was held, I wasn't surprised that his pastor was conducting the service. But what did surprise me was that CNN televised it live. In the Indianapolis Convention Center's lobby, just outside the doors that led to the auditorium for morning worship, four big televisions were mounted high above the doors, all tuned to different stations.

The TV on the end, the first one my husband and I came to, was tuned to CNN. After years of watching preaching on TV, I could tell by the way the gentleman pointed to his listeners, paused to check his notes, and then allowed his countenance to dissolve into a sweet smile that some serious preaching was going on there. Most of the people at the Praise Gathering were already in the auditorium, but a few latecomers, like David and me, were still in the lobby.

The television had caught our eye not because it was loud but because of the words at the bottom of the screen. The closed-captioning was on, and the word *heaven* had snagged my attention, so I stopped to read.

AND THEN PAYNE ARRIVED AT THE GATE

AND JUST ON THE OTHER SIDE

HE COULD SEE THE MOST BEAUTIFUL GOLF COURSE

HE HAD EVER SEEN.

HE SAW A GATEKEEPER AT THE ENTRANCE

AND ASKED, "CAN ANYONE PLAY ON THIS COURSE?"

AND THE GATEKEEPER ANSWERED, "YES. ANYONE WHO ASKS MAY PLAY THIS COURSE."

AND PAYNE SMILED AND ASKED, "AND HOW MUCH WILL IT COST ME TO PLAY HERE?"

THE GATEKEEPER SMILED BACK AND TOLD PAYNE, "IT WILL COST YOU NOTHING."

AND PAYNE ASKED, "HOW CAN THAT BE? IT IS SUCH A MAGNIFICENT COURSE."

AND THE GATEKEEPER SAID, "I HAVE ALREADY PAID THE PRICE FOR YOU."

AND PAYNE ASKED THE GATEKEEPER, "JUST HOW MUCH DID IT COST YOU?"

AND THE GATEKEEPER ANSWERED, "EVERYTHING."

The words scrolled up slowly, sometimes misspelled, sometimes with the *a*'s and *the*'s left out, but David and I read along, each of us mouthing the words, barely whispering them. I began to weep as the preacher on the TV continued his message, describing Payne Stewart in paradise, playing on a course bought and paid for with a great sacrifice. When I turned to wipe my eyes, I noticed others in the lobby, staring at the same screen, lips barely moving, some dabbing at their eyes, all soaking in the wonder of God.

Just beyond the doors were more than twelve thousand people worshiping in song, a song muffled by the closed doors. But out here, in the nearly empty lobby, God spoke out in the silence, through big, block letters that moved slowly across a TV screen. I thought of Elijah, who strained to hear God in the thunder and in the fire only to hear his whisper in the calm.

During three days filled with booming voices, shrill voices, laughing voices, and singing voices, with guitars, drums, cymbals, and one banjo, *that* was the loudest moment for me. God speaks to us all the time, in so many ways. But we must uncover our ears and listen—or at least read the closed-captioning.

Noisy Mimes in Indianapolis

Dancing in the Living Room

Let them praise his name with dancing and make
music to him with tambourine and harp.

PSALM 149:3

I was born to dance. Whenever I hear music, my toes tap in
time all by themselves. Sometimes it doesn't even have to be
music that makes them do that. Once I put a pair of sneakers in the dryer, and they got to tumbling round and round
and making a pretty cool beat, and I didn't think I was ever
going to get the dishes done!

For most people this gift (or curse) wouldn't be such a
problem, but I grew up a preacher's daughter in the South
in a denomination that told us as far back as I can remember
that dancing was a no-no.

"But David danced all the time in the Psalms," I told my parents after my knowledge of the Old Testament grew.

"And David got in a lot of trouble," my parents responded.

Dancing was out of the question in my house. God and dancing just didn't go together. So I had to make my feet stay still.

I grew up, got married (to a David—only he didn't dance), and went to work in a country music theme park in Nashville. One day we were rehearsing a big dance number we were supposed to do right in the middle of the show. I couldn't believe it! I was finally going to dance. The band played this fast bluegrass number with fiddles, mandolins, and drums, and my feet just took off.

About halfway through the day, the instructor called me over. "Girl, you have a real nice voice. You sing so pretty. But to be honest with you, you can't dance a lick."

But I already had bought my dance shoes! What was I supposed to do?

"We do something right after the dance number that maybe you'd be interested in," the instructor continued. "Have you ever heard of Cousin Minnie Pearl?"

So I turned in my dancing shoes for a pair of patent-leather flats, a gingham dress, and a straw hat with a price tag on it and told jokes for about fifteen minutes five times a day, every day, for six days a week—while everyone else got to dance.

The years passed, and I told fewer Minnie Pearl jokes and more of my own. People would call me from all over the country and ask me to come tell jokes, but no one ever asked me to dance—until one evening when my husband was surfing through the channels and came across a ballroom dance competition.

"Wow!" I heard him call from the sofa. "Isn't that the sort of dancing you were wanting to do?"

I stood there staring at the television, clutching the dishtowel, and dreaming. "Yes," I answered, kind of breathy like.

"Looks easy," was all David said.

"That's because they're so good," I said.

He studied the moves for a moment. "Nah, it's pretty easy. I mean, look, one-two-three, step, turn. One-two-three and turn. Now twirl and dip. Easy."

"Please take me sometime," I begged into the dishtowel.

"I'll take you right now." He stood up and offered his hand—the way the male contestants did on TV—and invited me onto the living-room dance floor. "Stand back, children," he warned Zach, who was four, and Chera, who was nine. "Your mother and I are about to win first place." He placed one hand on my hip and clasped my other hand in his while I placed one hand on his shoulder and giggled.

He stared me straight in my eyes and sort of smiled, but I could tell he was mostly counting—and concentrating. One-two-three, step, turn, and he pushed off my hip and twirled me like a top with his other hand. Chera clapped, and Zachary squealed. One-two-three, step, turn, and he twirled me again.

"Oops," I whispered, as I brushed against the sofa. "Watch out for the couch." One-two-three, step, and turn and dip—

That's all I remember. The rest of this story I'll have to pass along to you secondhand since I was knocked out.

Dancing in the Living Room

"When I tried to dip you," David told me later at my bedside (I thought it was so sweet of him to carry me all the way from the living room), pressing a cold rag to my forehead, "I couldn't make up my mind to do a really big dip or just a little one."

"Looks like you chose the big one," I said.

"I know, I know, but not on purpose," he said. "And I'm sorry. But you just slipped right out of my arms, landed flat on your back—except for your head, which smashed into the sofa, that hard part right on the end." Then he acted out, in slow motion, how my head hit the sofa and recoiled like a rubber ball against a street curb. "And did you ever hit it hard," he added. "WHACK!" And he smacked his hands together. "At first you just laid there and smiled at me, so precious, so sweet, like an angel. That's when I believed everything would be okay. But then your eyes rolled back enough to make Zachary scream, so Chera called 9-1-1. I patted your cheek, like this." He tapped me a couple of times, and I felt my head throb. "I was afraid to move your head, in case your neck was broken."

"That's very thoughtful," I said.

"I saw that on TV—not on the dance show, though. Some mountain rescue show, I believe. But you were only out about fifteen seconds. When you sat up, I knew your neck wasn't broken." David smiled because he had guessed right. "Oh, and the couch is just fine."

"Good," I answered. "I'd hate for anything to happen to that."

"I guess that's why they call it *ballroom* dancing," he said. "Because you're supposed to do it in a ballroom, not in a living room full of furniture. It's probably real easy to do in a ballroom."

For all the falling and crashing and whacking, I came away with only a big knot on the back of my head. A blessed woman, I guess. After that, I tried not to pay any attention to the beat of the washing machine. (I let the sneakers dry out in the sun.) I even blocked all the TV stations that might show dance competitions.

I was trying to be so good, but then I read about dancing just the other day—in Psalms!—about how David danced before the Lord. And he sang, laughed, raised his arms and—and I realized that God was even there, in the dancing!

Maybe if I wore a helmet . . .

Dancing in the Living Room

You Can't Grow Macaroni

Then he said to them, "Give to Caesar what is
Caesar's, and to God what is God's."

MATTHEW 22:21

The soapsuds rise up from the bottom of the tub and cover
me like a warm quilt. Oh, if Calgon could really take me
away, I'd curl up on my grandmother's sofa in front of her
roaring fireplace as she tucks the corners of one of her tat-
tered-piece quilts around my feet. But try as I might, I have
to settle for a small reprieve in my tub, hidden away for just
a moment.

A few days ago, while standing in the line at the grocery
store, I had read that placing slices of cucumbers over your

eyes would make them look five years younger. I'm so desperate, I decided to try it! Now, the cucumbers lie cool and heavy, like quarters, on my eyelids. I can't help but chuckle to myself because Mom said carrots were supposed to help my eyes. We had the wrong vegetable all along!

Maybe I should have finished reading the magazine article, because then I would know how you're supposed to keep the veggies from sliding off your eyelids.

I let my arms float up by my sides. My eyes are closed now, and when I try to open them, all I see is a green light filtered through the cucumber slices. So I close them tighter and begin to think about Chera, our fifteen-year-old daughter—the one who wants to be a missionary.

She knew she wanted to be a missionary when she was ten. I remember the night the drama troupe came to church, and at the end of their program they invited young people who have a heart for missions to come forward so some of the performers could pray with them. That's when little Chera made a beeline to the front. Zach was only five, and when he saw Chera go forward, he whispered to me, "I want to be a missionary too."

"You do?" I asked.

He nodded. Then as everyone prayed for the future missionaries, he leaned in close to me and asked, "What's a missionary?"

But Chera never wrestled with that question. She seemed always to have known what a missionary is and what a missionary does. In turn, I've always been concerned she isn't tough enough, that her heart is way too tender.

Why, when she was three, every time we went to the video store, she wanted to rent *Pinocchio* the cartoon. And every time she watched the circus master lock Pinocchio in a cage, when all Pinocchio wanted to do was go home to his father, Chera cried. "This is a sad story," she would say, wiping her eyes with the heel of her hand.

When she was older, maybe ten, she cried the first time she heard the DC Talk song "What If I Stumble?" already feeling the burden of presenting herself as a witness.

I wish I could soak in a tub all day and act as if nothing were going to change. But it won't work. I know because I already tried, and in a blink she went from collecting bugs in the backyard to perusing college catalogs. Some moments I wish I could freeze-frame, like when Chera was so excited to learn that some of her favorite things to eat grew on plants—like tomatoes and green beans. But she was tremendously disappointed to learn that macaroni wasn't a plant.

At first I believed her idea to be a missionary was one of those wishes that changes with each birthday. You know, like a child wanting to be president of the United States one day and a cashier at the corner 7-11 the next. For heaven's sake, when she was five, all she would talk about was getting her own gas station!

But when Chera paid more and more attention to maps and stories of far-off countries in missions magazines, I thought to myself, *Thank goodness nothing is set in stone when you're ten!* Five years have passed since then. And the conversations are still the same. Her room is filled with books of missionaries living in "the bush," battling (sometimes to the death) disease, sickness, irreverent and harassing governments, and hunger.

The harshest of these stories have done nothing to dissuade her. Sometimes I catch her with a book about the life of a missionary lying open before her as she daydreams about mango trees and fresh lion tracks in the village.

Lately she's been receiving a lot of mail from universities across the country. Dutifully she studies the catalogs, flipping past the colorful photos of grinning, laughing students having fun in the student center or couples meandering hand-in-hand along sidewalks through an autumn landscape (those PR people sure are good). But Chera heads straight for the curriculum sections.

Dreamy eyed, she studies the third-world curriculum offered by each institution. "Look, Mom," she says, pointing to a section of small print in the middle of a page. "You're required to take two semesters of African culture studies. *Required!* Can you believe it?"

I just nod, trying to look interested. Trying not to weep, as my little girl gets excited about going to a country on the other side of the world.

I wonder about Abraham and Isaac. I don't believe Isaac had a clue about what was going on as he headed up that mountain to be sacrificed, but I do believe he desired to please his father. "Here, Dad," he might have said. "Give me the twine, and I'll tie up my legs, then you can get more wood for the fire."

I can imagine Abraham's heart breaking in two as he prepared to offer his only child—a child so long in coming—to God.

I take a deep breath, and the quilt of bubbles starts to sink into the cooling water. No one has banged on the door yet to disturb my solitude with a life-shattering question such as, "Mom, where is the peanut butter?" So I stay put a little longer and try to figure out where in the world fifteen years went.

A few months ago, Chera and I traveled to Guatemala with a group from World Vision. I wanted to guard Chera's heart. If she cried at Pinocchio in a cage, I was sure she would weep at the poverty and deprivation we would witness in Guatemala. She didn't weep; instead, she studied every story, every landscape, every detail—she soaked it all in.

And she laughed. Not at anyone or anything, but *with* the children. She held the tiny ones; she sang with others; she played soccer in the village streets with giggling children all around, who were mesmerized by her blonde hair blowing in the wind. (Very few of those children had ever seen blonde hair.) One by one she touched each child that came near her and sat still while they slowly reached up to touch her strangely colored locks of hair. She made the children laugh when she called out, "*¡Escuche pepino!*" which means, "Listen to the cucumber!" It was the only Spanish phrase she knew. (*VeggieTales* doesn't exactly prepare you for international travel.)

I watched love and laughter spill out of my daughter, splashing over onto those "unfortunate" children and dousing them all so that they glowed.

Maybe, I thought, *this fanciful notion of being a missionary will pass now that we've traveled out of the country and the romance of the idea has been stripped away.* At least that's what I thought until I received an e-mail from Chera only a few weeks before her fifteenth birthday. She should have been concerned about the party, the invitations, the silly boys at school. But no.

Her e-mail was about Mauritania, one of the most desolate countries in the world, she was quick to tell me. She had done some research on the internet and discovered that only about ten thousand people live in this western coastal country in Africa. Very few areas have running water or utilities. It is dry and dusty and only a couple of degrees away from qualifying as a desert. And that is where she says she wants to go.

What am I supposed to do? Go find more firewood while she binds the cords tighter around her own limbs? No matter what we see or how much time passes, that once fanciful dream of a ten-year-old isn't going away.

My desire always has been that she know God. I desire nothing less than that she have a happy and loving relationship with God the Father. But how can I keep these crazy notions of trotting the globe so she can spread the gospel out of her head?

And it seems for her the more dangerous the situation, the better. She wanted to go to China last summer to smuggle Bibles. Do you know how many Bibles you can hide in a trunk with a false bottom? Chera knows.

As I watch her growing, reading, studying (lying on that altar), I realize I can't stop her.

"Mother, I can't wait to take them some hope," she told me, referring to the people of Mauritania. "They need it."

Sometimes I think it would be so much easier to give my child to God if she were a drug addict or an alcoholic. It would be so much easier for me to say, "Here, God, take her. I can't do a thing with her, but maybe you can." Then when anyone would ask, I would say, "Well, she's in God's hands now."

Don't misunderstand me. I know this missionary dilemma is a different burden than the burden many parents carry for their children. I met a pastor's wife in San Diego who shared with me about her son, who not only had been addicted to drugs but also was selling them. She said, "You can't imagine what it's like to answer the front door one morning and see an FBI agent standing there. He tells you the most frightening stories about your son. The same son who has just graduated with honors. All you can do is give him to the Lord. It's out of your hands at that point."

Out of my hands. That's what frightens me. Sometimes I find myself thinking, *But if I give her to him now, he might take her away. And that just doesn't seem fair.*

The water is no longer cooling—it's cold. I can hear the muffled sound of children's voices creeping closer to the door, the sound of a glass tipping over on the coffee table, and the sound of David stomping past with a slight huff— you know, the how-long-are-you-going-to-be-in-there huff.

I lift the stopper and the water escapes, making a gurgling sound. I look for the cucumbers, worried I might have a real maintenance problem on my hands. I find one stuck to the soap bar and the other stuck to the side of my Tweety Bird sponge. (Don't ask.) I drop the slices on the floor, praying that at least a couple of years have just dropped with them.

As I listen to the sounds of the water leaving, I think again about Mauritania. Maybe Chera never will go there. Maybe God merely has sent along a catalog so she can peruse the curriculum, familiarize herself with the courses available so she can be an advisor to would-be missionaries.

Now, wrapped in my tattered terrycloth robe, I dry my hair and make myself pray that Chera learns all she needs to know to survive in a place like Mauritania, since it looks as if I'm losing the battle to keep her here. She knows that God is real, that he loves her, and that he guides her steps. She knows I wish she would stay always with me. But I know in her heart there rests a desire not just to stand in the gap but to fill it in with the words of the gospel, to see more children laughing like those in Guatemala. (Why did I ever take her?)

"Do you know how many people immigrate to Mauritania every year?" she asked me one day shortly after the e-mail. Then without waiting for an answer, she said, "Zero." And she made a zero by touching her thumb to her middle finger. Then she added, "You know they speak French there." (She's taking French in high school. She loves to point out God's hand at work.) "It's dry and dusty, and they farm for a living. It's perfect."

Farm? I remember Chera's knowledge of farming, how surprised she was to discover that tomatoes and green beans grow on plants. I turn off the blow dryer and continue my long conversation with God. Suddenly, a swelling sense of peace that she will be all right covers me. And I didn't even have to hold cucumbers on my eyes. I sense his presence, I hear his voice, as he reminds me that he is God, and I am mom.

While I brush through my hair, I hear him gently say, "She'll be okay, Chonda. I will watch her every move. Besides, she already knows you can't *grow* macaroni and cheese."

chapter
24

The Septic Tank Man

This is the day the LORD has made; let us rejoice
and be glad in it.

PSALM 118:24

Someone told David and me that if we were going to build
a cabin in the woods we would need a septic tank.

"In the woods? Are you sure?" David said, and I couldn't
tell if he was more surprised or disappointed. But our friend
just nodded, and David could only shake his head sorrow-
fully.

It's funny how men and women think differently on cer-
tain subjects. Me? I was thinking septic tank from the day
David drove us to the top of the wooded hill and said, "Here.
Right here is where I want to build the first cabin." There in

161

the middle of the trees, undergrowth, and buzzing mosqui-toes, I was envisioning sparkling porcelain—and hand soap.

You see, a dream of ours is beginning to come true. We're building a retreat center for preachers' kids. We have seventy acres of hills with so many trees that if we want to put up even a storage shed, we have to lop down a gaggle (is that the right word?) of trees just to make room.

"This will be the front porch," David stood sideways and waved his arms as if he were guiding a 747 to its parking blocks. "And back there," he pointed to a stump, "is where the fireplace will be. And over there—"

"What about the toilet?" I interrupted.

"Toilet?" He wrinkled his brow.

Why had he repeated *toilet* as if I had spoken Portuguese?

"Yes, the toilet," I said. "With a bath and running water."

He studied the imaginary layout for a moment, one hand rubbing his chin thoughtfully before pointing to one spot on the ground and then another in the invisible cabin, naming each one as he went. "Spot for fireplace. Spot for sofa. Spot for La-Z-Boy. Spot for fishing pole rack. Spot for refrigerator to keep the fishing bait in. Hmmm. I guess, if we had to, we could squeeze in a toilet right over there." He pointed to an area next to his fishing pole rack. "Although that takes away from—"

"Perfect." I walked over to the area, as if staking that claim not only for myself but also for all women who might pass through this place (no pun intended).

Over the next few months, David met with the roadmen, the electricians, the builders, and the well driller. Each time he would meet with someone new, he would point to squares of ground just as he had with me and explain what was sup-posed to go there.

When each worker returned, he brought along tools that would either dig, cut, trench, or scrape. Before long, I was beginning to see the cabin my husband had described to me while I picked off ticks and slapped away mosquitoes as we stood among the gaggle (sure that's the right word?) of trees.

Finally, the grand day came. "I'm meeting with the septic tank man," David announced to me one morning as he laced up his boots to head to the woods. "Want to come?"

"Sure," I sang. I wouldn't normally sing about septic tanks. Neither would I normally want to talk shop with a septic tank man, but I felt a lot was at stake here: every preacher's kid's comfort and mine. I would go for the cause.

The smells of cedar and oak pollen, concrete, freshly dug dirt, and insect repellant mingled in the forest air. The Septic Tank Man pulled up in a truck as big as a tank, climbed down, and shook David's hand. (At first I was a bit concerned about that, but I had to remind myself that the tanks were *clean* concrete shells when he installed them.) He was a big man with a dark tan and a beaming smile, and he introduced himself as Spencer.

After he and David stomped around a bit, Spencer pointed to some trees behind the cabin site and said, "I guess right in there will work just fine."

"Well, it is downhill." David chuckled.

Spencer chuckled back and pretended that was the first time he had heard that one. "Well, you guys are going to have a nice place here."

"It's for preachers' kids," David blurted.

Spencer raised his eyebrows, so David explained how tough it is in the world of ministry, how people who are trying to spread the gospel and make this a better world are often the ones so beaten down, but there's nowhere for them to go. Maybe if they just had a place to hike through shady woods, stare at a tree crafted by the greatest Artist, or watch a deer drink from a river—maybe a place like that would rest their souls, would allow them to see the handiwork of a God who loved them. "A place like that is what we're trying to build," David explained.

Spencer nodded, grinned his bright smile, and added, "There's a lot of trouble in this world." Every word was heavy with experience. "Seven years ago I got shot."

Shot? What? Why? Where? Bank robbery? Prison riot? Drive-by? Accident? Duel? What if someone was still after him?

I spied a gaggle of trees close by and decided I would run there to hide, if necessary. So much was running through my mind, and it seemed a lot was working its way through David's too.

Spencer must have noticed and went on to explain. "I was working late one night when a couple of teenagers broke in and one of them shot me with a shotgun." With that, Spencer pulled the neck of his T-shirt down and let us see the jagged scar that started at the base of his neck and disappeared out of view down his shirt.

"I thought I was going to die," he continued. "It felt like I was stuck up on the ceiling, and I could see myself lying on the floor, bloody and dying. But my baby girl had been born the week before, and I guess God wasn't ready for me to die just yet. So I came off the ceiling and went back into my body and dragged myself down the road to a house for help. I was in the hospital for weeks."

I felt awful for having thought he might be a bad guy.

"Yeah, a lot of crazy people are around, and a lot of crazy stuff goes on in this world," he went on. (I thought about some of the e-mail I get from preachers' kids and quietly agreed.) "You guys are doing a good thing."

Then he paused long enough to let that big, porcelain smile of his spread across his suntanned face. "But I tell you what. *Every* day for me," and now he opened up his arms as if to embrace the whole world, "is a good day!" His smile was the biggest it had been yet.

So there we stood on the hill, with Spencer's giant smile and the aroma of fresh dirt in the air, surrounded by a gaggle of trees, while our Septic Tank Man gave praise to God with outstretched arms. Not even the talk of a padded seat could have made me any happier.

Suddenly, I wished there was a song about the Septic Tank Man (I made a mental note to talk to some of my songwriting friends when I got back home) because I wanted to sing one. I wanted to sing one because I didn't think we could have found a better septic tank man in the whole county—the whole world!

Spencer opened my eyes to the wonderfulness of being here and being alive. I don't believe I'll ever be able to flush again without being reminded that *every day* is a good day.

I Think I Just Locked My Keys in the Car

He got up, rebuked the wind and said to the waves, "Quiet! Be still!" Then the wind died down and it was completely calm.

MARK 4:39

I've locked the keys in my car many times—many, *many* times if David were to tell you. But this one particular time, David and the children were there to share in the experience. Once airport security, a professional locksmith, and shortly after that the police showed up, we had a nice little storm brewing in the parking garage.

David and Chera had been out climbing a mountain (a new activity of theirs) and were planning to take a shuttle to the parked car once they returned. But I figured Zach and I would meet them at the gate to surprise them.

I especially wanted to surprise David with a gift a close friend had given us. It was in my car's trunk, and I just knew David would love it: a stained glass window for the cabin we were building in the woods.

So when I picked them up at the airport, I showed it to David right away. "You like it?" I wafted my arms toward the small window in the trunk much like those too tall, too skinny girls do on *The Price Is Right* as they point to a box of macaroni.

"I love it," he said. "It's one of my favorite scenes from the Bible."

I love surprises.

"I'm starved," said Zach. "Can we get something to eat?"

"Okay, let's go!" I stopped wafting my arms, slammed the trunk closed, and brushed garage dust from my hands—my *empty* hands.

David must have read my mind because he asked, "Did you just lock your keys in the trunk?"

I checked my empty pockets and nodded sadly. "I think so."

"Oops," Chera chirped.

"Does this mean we're not going to get something to eat?" asked Zach.

"Let me think." David pulled on the locked car handles, tugging on each one again and again. He squeezed the trunk latch, pushed against the sunroof, and then leaned over the windshield and tried to push down the electric lock button inside the car by using the power of his mind. Nothing happened.

While David tried to mentally zap open the car, I flagged down the airport security truck that was making its round through the garage. An older fellow with a big belly hopped out of the cab. He was holding a long, flat, metal bar in one hand.

"I see this all the time," he growled, moving straight to my car.

"Oh, good," I said. "I mean, it's not good that people lock the keys in their cars, but it's good that you've done something like this before."

He stopped just short of my car and looked it over from bumper to bumper. "Hmm," he said. "I don't think I've done one of *these* before."

But that didn't slow him down. He shoved the metal bar between the glass and doorframe and jiggled the bar up and down and back and forth.

David was still moving around the car, studying the seams, trailing a finger along the bumper and the taillights.

The man with the big belly jiggled the bar for about fifteen minutes. Sweat beaded on his forehead and dripped onto the side glass.

Chera had settled onto her bag and was into a round of some game on Zach's Game Boy.

Zach got tired of watching the sweaty, jiggling man and said, "Why don't we just bust out the glass and press the button?"

The jiggly man stopped. "Are these electronic locks?"

"Yes," I answered.

He mopped his brow with a handkerchief he had pulled from his back pocket. "I think you're going to need a locksmith. This is a bit too sophisticated for me."

He made the call for us, and in a few minutes another truck showed up. This man was older and had a big belly too.

I Think I Just Locked My Keys in the Car

He pulled out a small, boxlike contraption with wires, cords, and cables shooting out from all sides. On the back of this box was a big suction cup. He slapped the contraption down on top of the car, and the suction cap made a smacking sound like a big kiss.

"Cool!" said Zach.

Chera looked up for a moment, a bit concerned, then returned to her game.

David watched as the professional grabbed hold of one of the legs sprouting from the box and shoved it between the doorframe and glass where the jiggly man had worked so hard earlier. We found out right away that one of the box's wiry arms was a bright light that made the whole car glow in the dark garage—like an angel car. Chera paused her game and watched; Zach shielded his eyes. But when the professional jiggled his wires and cables and started to sweating, David went back to pushing and prodding on all the locked doors and windows.

"I still say we bust out the window," said Zach. His idea was sounding better.

The professional stopped trying to hide his frustration. He rubbed his chin, jiggled his contraption harder, and even tried turning the light on and off a few times. Nothing.

Zach was slumped over the hood, starvation wreaking its savage effects upon his ten-year-old body. Chera was slumped against one of the garage columns, channeling all her energy into mashing the proper Game Boy buttons. Then David announced, "I'm going in."

Chera stopped her game. Zach rose up from the car hood. I gasped and put a hand to my mouth. The professional with the super flashlight stopped jiggling, and we all looked at David.

I Can See Myself in His Eyeballs

"You're going to bash in the window?" Zach asked hopefully.

David sauntered to the back of the car, moving slowly like he had been all evening, knelt behind the car, and placed both hands on the left taillight.

"The keys are in the trunk, right?" he asked me.

I nodded.

"Then I'm going in right here." He tapped the taillight. He turned to the professional locksmith. "Excuse me, mister, but may I borrow some tools?"

"For smashing?" Zach asked.

The locksmith dug around in his toolbox, pulled out a small crowbar, and handed it to David.

"All right!" Zach shouted, running around behind the car. "Can I have a swing?"

As David worked the crowbar into the seam around the light, a police officer stepped up. "Excuse me, ma'am, but did you sign a waiver with that man in case he tears something up?"

"As a matter of fact, I married him."

The officer blushed and said, "Oh, well, I guess that's waiver enough."

Chera laid down her game and, along with Zach, the professional locksmith, the police officer, and me, made a semicircle around the back of the car, watching David pry, twist, jiggle, and finally smash out the back taillight.

CRASH!

"All right!" shouted Zach.

"Cool," said Chera.

"Well, I'll be," said the professional, wrapping up his suction-cupped, tentacled box.

I Think I Just Locked My Keys in the Car

"This *is* your car, ma'am, isn't it?" the officer asked officially.

Zach was the only one who could reach into the small hole. He shoved his arm in up to his shoulder and fished around until his tiny fingers found the lost keys. He grinned as he pulled them free. "*Now* can we eat?" he asked.

I opened the trunk to put in the broken taillight pieces and looked at the stained glass window that, in some way, had started this whole storm. But I was reminded of a peace and a calm that comes straight from heaven. For there, in my trunk, was a brilliant image (without the aid of any fancy locksmith light) of an old fishing boat draped in fishing nets, resting on a peaceful shore.

"Quiet, be still," Jesus had spoken from a similar boat in the midst of a different storm. I couldn't wait to build our cabin around this window and to be reminded daily of a Master who commands the wind and the waves.

We got something to eat that night, so no one starved. We gave the professional locksmith twenty dollars for his time (we figured that would help to pay his light bill), and we assured the uniformed officer that this was indeed our car and that, really, Officer, there was no need to file a report.

But more important, I was reminded that peace, rest, is available in the midst of the storm, in the midst of something as frustrating as locking your keys in the car, even in the midst of professionals with bright lights and big bellies who jiggle in dark parking garages. It's the peace that comes from gazing into God's eyeballs.

All the Ice Cream You Can Eat

Be merciful, just as your Father is merciful.

LUKE 6:36

The Chattanooga Choo-Choo is a famous hotel about one hundred miles from where we live. It used to be an old train depot at which people caught rides to Nashville or up to Knoxville or down to Atlanta. Now it's a grand hotel with restaurants, shops, gardens, swimming pools, and little chocolate mints that somehow appear on your pillow just before bedtime. It's a grand place, indeed.

And this is a story about how one day it almost became the Chonda-nooga Choo-Choo. I think that has a nice ring to it, don't you?

That weekend was our daughter's twelfth birthday. I was scheduled to appear at the Comedy Catch, a genuine comedy club with neon beer signs and ashtrays. But the night I was performing was family night—no alcohol or smoking allowed (so all the Baptists could see what a den of iniquity looked like!). We decided to take the kids along, spend a couple of extra days at the Choo-Choo, and go to the aquarium in town.

Zachary was six and learning to swim, so all he was interested in was hitting the pool. "When can we go swimming?" he asked, crawling out of the car after we parked in front of the hotel lobby.

"First, we need to check in," I said, helping David to wiggle some of the luggage out of the trunk.

"So when can we swim?" asked Zach.

"It's *my* birthday," said Chera.

"Don't you want to swim on your birthday?" Zach cooed, as if this were his special gift to her.

"Let's get checked in first," said David. "We'll go up to the room, make sure we have ESPN, *then* we'll find the pool."

"But it's *my* birthday," said Chera.

"Okay," said David, "then *you* check to see if they have ESPN."

We finally moved everything into the room. Zach was half-naked by the time we got there and dug through the suitcase for his swim trunks while David surfed through the channels. Since I had to work that night, I began to pull my comedy clothes out of the suitcase. (The club's owner was even going to cover up the neon Budweiser sign.)

"Can we go swimming now?" Zach stood in the middle of the room (but not in front of the TV set) with his swim trunks on backward.

The plan was for the children to swim for about an hour. David and I would sit and watch from the side of the pool, like I'd seen the old folks do when I was growing up. Now I realized that some of those people didn't refrain from swimming because they were so old but because, maybe, some of them had to work in a comedy club in an hour.

A huge slide at the indoor pool looped around a couple of times before dropping off into the deep end. Of course, that's where Zach ran first thing. "Happy birthday, Chera!" he yelled as he circled around some fake trees and real rocks and splashed into the water. Then he dog-paddled to the edge and pulled himself up.

He did that a couple of times before he screamed so loud it shook the teeth in my head. From where I was, he seemed to be okay, because he was hanging onto the side of the pool, his body in the water and his elbows propped up on dry ground.

At first I thought maybe he had come up with another birthday cheer for Chera, you know, "Yeeeeooohhh! Happy birthday, Chera! Yeeeoowww!!!" But he just kept screaming, like one of those kids in the *Jaws* movie who hangs onto a capsized catamaran with both hands while kicking away at a thirty-foot shark with his feet. Something wasn't right.

"Pick him up!" I yelled at David.

David snatched him from the water and slung him onto the indoor-outdoor carpet that covered the area. Blood went everywhere.

"He's bleeding," I said. I probably should have yelled, but I was in shock, like the mother in the movie *Jaws* who's watching her son hang onto that catamaran.

"He's bleeding bad," said David. "His foot, I think."

All the Ice Cream You Can Eat

"But it's *my* birthday," said Chera from the top of the slide.

We wrapped up Zach's foot in a pool towel and didn't worry about the stain it would leave. Chera volunteered to tell someone. She ran, all wet and drippy, to the front desk and made sure she mentioned something about a "child" and "bleeding like a stuck pig" (the things she picks up from her father!). In two seconds the manager, the maintenance man, housekeeping, and a gardener were all by the poolside checking on little Zachary's foot.

"It's cut pretty deep," said the manager, holding Zach's tiny foot. "I'll call an ambulance." He was on his radio in a second. The maintenance man had rolled up his sleeve and was checking along the poolside for what might have done this. Around one of the light fixtures he found a loose screw, backed out about a half-inch, as long and as sharp as a shark's tooth.

"This is pretty dangerous," the maintenance man said to all of us, as he rubbed his hand over the sharp screw.

The manager's face turned pale, and he checked on his radio to see how much longer the ambulance would be. Then he seemed to almost lose his balance (pass out?) before he said, "I'll take you myself."

Chera wrapped up in a couple of extra pool towels, and we all took a trip to the emergency room in a big, fine car— David, Chera, Zach, me, and the manager of the Chattanooga Choo-Choo.

Zach was a trooper the whole time. When he saw the giant needle, he let out another big birthday whoop, but once his foot went numb, he started to whistle and tell us all how much it didn't hurt a bit. When the doctor was finished,

Zach had twelve stitches on the bottom of his foot, starting at his big toe.

"And it's my twelfth birthday," said Chera. She was starting to think this was a pretty exciting birthday after all.

Zach made us all touch his stitches, and then he told us he couldn't feel a thing.

"Don't worry," said the doctor, who earlier had waved the giant needle around like a wand, "you will soon."

"That's okay, Zach," David tried to make him feel better. "At least now you can have all the ice cream you want."

"Really?" he said.

I looked at David, but he nodded his head firmly.

The Chattanooga Choo-Choo manager, still sort of pale, nodded too.

Now that everything was all sewn up, the manager insisted we could leave Zach and Chera at the hotel, and he would check on them personally while I went and did a quick set at the beerless comedy club. A big vase of flowers was waiting for me when I arrived at the club, compliments of the Choo-Choo.

When we left Zach, he was in bed with his bandaged foot propped up on a couple of pillows, remote control in hand. Chera was in the chair by his side. When we returned, we found the room filled with balloons, a couple of big baskets of candies and toys from the downstairs gift shop, some coloring books on the nightstand by Zach's bed, and two big bowls that used to have ice cream in them. Zach was watching the Cartoon Channel and had the remote control resting on his belly (hereditary, maybe), and Chera was fluffing the pillows that held up his foot. King Zachary!

All the Ice Cream You Can Eat

"What's all this?" I asked Zachary, waving a hand over the balloons and toys.

"All of this is for my sore toe," said Zach.

"They just keep sending up stuff," said Chera, smiling.

"The man said to just call him if we needed anything," explained Zach. "Watch this." Zachary picked up the phone, punched zero, and when someone answered said, "Yes, can you bring up some more ice cream, please? *Two* bowls again because today is my sister's birthday." Then he hung up. "See?"

I thought for a moment before saying, "Let me see that menu."

Soon we had more ice cream, hot wings, cheeseburgers, and spinach dip than any of us could eat. For the rest of the night we watched cartoons, ate, and took turns looking at Zachary's stitches.

"It hurts a little bit now," said Zachary just before we went to bed.

"Fluff up his pillows," Chera instructed, speaking from experience. "That makes it feel better."

"Do you want some more ice cream?" a sleepy Zachary asked Chera.

"No, thanks," she answered.

"Because it's your birthday," said Zach.

Just before everyone fell asleep, full of ice cream, I heard David say to Zach, "Hey, Zach, are you finished with that remote control?"

The manager was glad to learn we wouldn't be filing any sort of claim against the hotel. I think that was the moment the color started to return to his face. We told him that, in spite of all the blood, the long needles, and the twelve stitches in Zach's foot, God sure had been watching out for us, because things could have been a lot worse. The manager just nodded, soaking in the relief, I guess.

We still remember that weekend—especially Zachary—and talk about it all the time. What we remember the most is the ice cream, the balloons, and the cartoons. I hope the manager remembers us too—not how we wiped out his ice cream supply but that we were a family who felt God had watched out for us, a family who was grateful for a trip to the emergency room in a nice car, for a doctor who could stitch up a big cut in a small toe, for big fluffy pillows, and for room service. Maybe he even understands why this family didn't sue the pants off him and his Chattanooga Choo-Choo!

The Christmas Surprise Surprise

This will be a sign to you: You will find a baby wrapped in cloths and lying in a manger.

Luke 2:12

Sometimes when I think about Christmas I think of a small, crowded shelter. I think of a noisy place full of different smells and fragrances, and of course, I think of surprises. No, I don't think I'll ever forget the Christmas with the little tent and the noisy perfume counter.

You see, one Christmas I wanted to surprise David with a tent so he could camp out in the woods where he could grow a beard, eat things that had turned black over the campfire, study his compass for hours on end to figure out where a certain tree was that he had tied an orange ribbon around earlier, breathe air full of mosquitoes, and run through forests laced with spider webs . . . anyway, that's why he wanted a tent.

The kids and I found one that folded down into a small but heavy package. It would fit nicely under one arm, to make it easier for him to trudge deep into the snake-infested woods.

So we bought the tent, wrapped it up, and set it under the tree.

No matter how much he shook it, he couldn't guess what it was. Finally he said to Zach, who was only five years old then, "Okay, I give up. What is it, Zachary?"

Zachary just shook his head defiantly, like we had practiced while we were wrapping, and said in a singsong way, "It's not a tent!"

There's nothing like being surprised by a surprise. Not that David was going to find out that Christmas . . .

That same Christmas, I was in another store, standing in line at a perfume counter (a store that obviously didn't sell tents) behind a tall, lanky young man who wore a ball cap that caused his long hair to curl up over his ears. He was sort of nervous and had a hard time pronouncing some of the French names on the bottles, so mostly he just pointed. He would take one of the bottles from the clerk, sniff, and ask the price.

"Now, this is our most popular fragrance this season." The clerk handed a tiny bottle to the young man, who pinched it between his thumb and forefinger. Then he screwed off the top and put his nose down to it like I've seen David do when testing a bottle of Tabasco sauce.

"Smells good," he said. "I think I'll take one of these."

"Good choice," responded the clerk. "That'll be sixty-four dollars."

"Sixty-four dollars!"

"Opium is a very popular brand."

The young man rubbed his chin, bit his lip, and scanned the rows of colored bottles on the shelves behind the clerk. "Do you have anything that smells sort of like Opium?" the young fellow asked.

The clerk rolled her eyes and put the Opium under the counter. "We have this." She clunked a large bottle filled with an orange liquid on the counter. "It smells like the expensive kind, but it's a lot cheaper."

The young man did a sniff test and seemed satisfied. "And how much is this?"

"It's seventeen dollars," she answered.

"Oh, wow, then give me *two* of them," said the young man.

The clerk bagged up two of the clunky bottles, and the young man, bottles tucked under his arm—as if they were a small tent—walked off with what was surely going to be one big surprise for some young lady.

I love a good surprise, whether it's a tent (or as Zach said, *not* a tent) or two gallons of a cheap perfume that smells expensive. A good surprise ought to knock you off your feet. It ought to make you cry, shout, jump, pump your fist in the air, sigh, turn green, punch the one you're with, and maybe even dance around in sheep doo-doo.

Let me explain that last part.

The greatest surprise I ever heard about took place at another Christmas, late one night in a rocky field. The night was probably cold, maybe even muddy, and no doubt a bit smelly—because of all the sheep.

The men in the field were shepherds, and all day they had kept the sheep moving, finding new grass to graze on. When one of the animals would stray, a shepherd would go after it and bring it back to the herd. At night the shepherds took turns sleeping and watching, "abiding by their flock," as the story goes.

But this particular night, they were in for a real surprise. I wonder if just one angel appeared at first, sort of like on the TV show in which the angel glows and says, "I've been sent by God." (I always cry when she glows like that.) Or if maybe they all (thousands, tens of thousands, hundreds of thousands—however many are in a host) appeared at once. Now that's what I call a surprise.

I imagine the sheep stayed put (another surprise!) while all the shepherds fell right down on the ground and stared in awe. When the heavenly host sang, I imagine some of the shepherds raised up on their elbows to listen. Some, the most awake among them, might have danced around (even though it was dark, muddy, and yucky). And I imagine those more familiar with the book of Isaiah even pumped their fists into the air and said, "Yes!"

Wow, did God ever surprise us big one year, not with a tiny tent or cheap bottles of perfume, but with a tiny manger filled with the Savior of the universe and the aroma of sheep, donkey, straw, and mud. What a surprise for a group of tired, smelly men who were simply watching their sheep.

What a surprise for all of us!

The Holy Ghost in New Orleans

> Blind Pharisee! First clean the inside of the cup
> and dish, and then the outside also will be clean.
>
> MATTHEW 23:26

For our seventeenth anniversary, David took me to the French Quarter in New Orleans.

"Excuse me?" I said, when David showed me the brochure of the French-sounding place we were staying. "New Orleans? The French Quarter? Mardi Gras? Plastic beads? I'm in the middle of writing a book about seeing God's presence all around and we're jetting off to New Orleans?"

"You like blues music, don't you?" he asked. "Well, this is where the blues was born."

"I like chocolate too," I answered, "but I don't care to go to a cocoa bean farm."

"Come on, look at it as a challenge. Besides, I have a feeling you're going to hear 'When the Saints Go Marchin' In' a million times, and that'll make a great chapter in your book."

So we went for three days—in the middle of summer! (That reminds me, I'm working on a new song—a blues number. So far I only have the title, "I've Got the It's-So-Hot-and-Humid-My-Face-Is-Melting-Off Blues." What do you think?)

A cab driver was our introduction to the city. He was a young, soft-spoken gentleman who seemed to know the town like the back of his hand.

"Excuse me," I asked from the backseat. "What is that building over there?" I pointed to a large stone building with a spire, flying buttresses, and stained glass.

"Oh, that's just some old church building," he said. I already had guessed that, but I thought maybe it was a famous church.

"Now, if you look down there," our driver continued, as he slowed enough so we could read the little storefront signs, "you'll see the Famous Door. They have two-for-one drinks until about nine o'clock. Then just past there is Pat O'Brien's. He's the one who invented the Hurricane. Three of those, and they'll have to drag you home."

"Or back to that big church we passed," I answered, a little upset that we were getting the grand imbibing tour.

"Yeah, I get it," he said. "A funeral! Ha ha!"

David laughed too.

I thought our hotel was very nice, very French, until a big, hairy fellow named Carlos escorted us to our room. "First time to New Orleans?" he asked.

We nodded.

"Oh, you're gonna love it! We have all kinds of shops and museums and restaurants and enough booze to float a battleship! Ha ha ha!"

When we arrived at the room, Carlos dragged in our luggage while David counted out his change for a tip. "Now, folks, I have to tell you something right up front," said Carlos, and my first thought was that maybe he was ill and he was telling us that he would no longer be able to act as our bellhop. "This is a very old building. And sometimes when they fix up these old buildings, there's a lot of extra walls." He walked over to the window and took hold of a corner of the curtain. "And if you're looking for a room with a view . . ." he yanked open the curtain to expose one of those extra walls he was talking about, so close to the window I could have reached out and touched it (very unlike the brochure David had shown me weeks earlier), "then this ain't it."

David shrugged. "We'll probably be out shopping anyway."

Carlos winked. "Make sure you get over to Cecil's—two for one all night."

David pressed some loose change into Carlos's palm, and Carlos smiled, barely.

Before he could leave I asked him, "What's that a picture of?" and pointed to the painting on our wall, the wall across from the one that was just outside our window.

Carlos took a look, as if it were the first time he'd ever seen it, and said, "Oh, that's the St. Louis Cathedral. About four blocks from here. The oldest cathedral in the United States. A beautiful place. You should check it out." Then he took his quarters and dimes and left.

David looked at me, and I raised my eyebrows.

"See?" he said. "This is going to make a great chapter."

Yes, this was indeed going to be a great chapter—I was determined. "Come on. We still have plenty of daylight left. Let's find that cathedral."

Our hotel was on Toulouse Street (very French). Carlos told us if we followed it all the way to the river, we would come to Jackson Square, where the St. Louis Cathedral was. So from our hotel we turned south and moved through the humidity, past the Priestess of the Dark Voodoo Shop, on past Big Daddy's Strip Club, just beyond the Funky Butt until we finally made it to Jackson Square, a very manicured park with beautiful flowers, shrubs, and statues.

The park and the church were surrounded by palm readers, tarot card readers, and even one young lady who flaunted her education. (The poster over her little table read "Psychology Major.") And there, at the end of the park, was the same image that hung on the wall of our hotel room: The St. Louis Cathedral.

We moved past the psychology major and into the somber cathedral. You could light a small candle for a dollar or a big candle for two dollars. David had some more loose change in his pocket—enough for a smaller candle—so I lit one.

We were in there for just a little while and then left. "Well?" David said to me as we walked back out into the heat. "Good?"

I knew that was his way of asking about the book. I just smiled and nodded. "Yes, real good." But I was worried about my chapter. The cathedral was nice, but I didn't notice anything but a lot of candle burning going on in there.

We walked on, past people who had painted their faces silver and who stood very, very still so that people walking by would drop money into a box. David had a quarter, and I was sure one of the living statues frowned when David dropped it in.

We stopped at a little cafe to eat beignets (a deep-fried pastry with about one box of powdered sugar dousing each one) and drink lattes when we heard a lone, sad trumpet playing "The Tennessee Waltz." (David exchanged a dollar bill for four quarters to cover all tips for our walk back.) Suddenly "The Tennessee Waltz" changed to "Amazing Grace." David poked me in the ribs, so we finished our beignets and followed the music.

Right outside we found the trumpeter, holding his trumpet with one hand and waving a brand-new CD with the other. He was an older black man with gray hair and very few teeth but a quick smile. His old trumpet case lay open on a table next to him, the velvet insides dirty and worn. An old, old Bible lay inside too.

When he saw us watching him, he waved us over. "You're going to like this." He handed David the CD. "These are all songs I wrote—except for 'Amazing Grace,' of course."

David studied the CD and said, "Interesting title here."

The trumpet player nodded and grinned. "That's right," he said. "You see, the Holy Ghost's done gone all through me!" and he waved his free hand over the top of his head and passed it all the way down to his feet.

"Wow, that sounds great!" David pulled out some paper money and paid the man for the CD. "Doesn't this sound great?" he asked me, showing me the CD so I could read the cover.

The Holy Ghost in New Orleans

I nodded.

"Here." The old man pulled a marker from his pocket and took the CD from David, tearing open the shrink-wrapping. "Let me sign it for you. Now, what's your name?" he asked me.

"It's Chonda," I said.

The old man paused with his pen just above the paper, looked at me, and said, "Chonda? Why, that was the very first word the Holy Spirit gave to me when I got my prayer language. I'd say it over and over and over before I got some more." Then he signed the CD for me, and we made our way back to the hotel—back past the St. Louis Cathedral, on past the tarot card readers, past the dancers, past the happy hours, proud to be carrying the latest, autographed copy of *The Holy Ghost Transfusion.*

God in New Orleans? Oh, yes. And I never really believed that he wouldn't be. Of course, he doesn't have a big storefront with a neon sign like most places there. And even though we never heard "When the Saints Go Marchin' In" even once, I believe he's at work there just like he is anywhere else—and with *anyone* else. And he works there in his favorite way: from the inside out.

The Blue Knight Picks My Daughter

How great is the love the Father has lavished on
us, that we should be called children of God!

1 JOHN 3:1

"What do you mean, we eat with our fingers?" I asked the
young waitress who stood before us and lowered a round
serving tray filled with four bowls of soup.

"There are no forks and spoons here at Medieval
Times," she said with a bouncy lilt to her voice, as she
passed out the bowls, "because there were no silver forks
and spoons in the year 1192." She tucked the tray under
her arm, smiled, and bounced away.

"There were no Medieval Times restaurants that
charged twenty-three fifty a plate to eat without silverware
either!" I called out after her, but I don't think she heard me.

"Maybe you should send her a note by carrier pigeon," David suggested, slurping his hot soup from the wooden bowl. He came up for air and said, "That's how they did it in medieval times."

Zach was only four years old then, but watching him and his father, their two faces buried in the bowls, their elbows flying out to the sides, it was hard to tell them apart. Even their slurping noises were identical.

Chera watched me as I picked up the bowl, extended my pinky, and began to slurp—I mean, sip. Chera did likewise. At least two of us would bring some class to this joint.

We were sitting in the front row of the blue section, next to the railing that was supposed to keep us from falling over onto the sawdust floor below where the battles between the knights would take place. All the romance of medieval times comes through clear and strong on TV and the big screen: the sleek horses, the full-flowing gowns and scarves, the ornate saddlery (that thing you strap onto the back of a horse). But in real life the romance gives way to the smells of those sleek horses, the bulkiness of the flowing gowns, and *no* silverware—and they still charged $23.50 a person!

We watched a rider on a horse run some figure eights around big red barrels while we slurped our soup, and then our bouncy waitress returned with the main course: turkey legs, one apiece. Zachary and David grunted and dived right in, faces first, into the greasy, blackened legs. Zachary grabbed the natural handle that the bone made, pointed at me with his dinner, and said, "This is great, Mom. Quit tearing off little pieces and eat it like mid-weevil times." Then he took too big of a bite and chewed on a hunk of meat that dangled out of the corner of his mouth.

I Can See Myself in His Eyeballs

The idea was disgusting, but the bony leg was the only handle we could find, so Chera and I each grabbed hold of a leg—pinkies out—and joined in the celebration.

On one end of the giant room, high above the sawdust floor and in a small box seat, the king sat alone. At one point he stood and announced it was time for the competition to begin. A group of knights, some wearing blue, some wearing red, some wearing yellow, and some wearing green, rode in on their horses. One brave knight from each color raced off on his horse to his respective colored section and, with a long spear, extended a same-colored scarf to someone in the section.

In our section, the blue knight extended the spear and scarf to Chera, my timid ten-year-old. Immediately she plopped her turkey leg onto her plate and, without any prompting from David or me, reached out with greasy fingers and removed the scarf from the spear point. The knight, with long, blonde hair and a matching goatee (way too old for my daughter), tipped his head in respect and told Chera he would return for her later. "Do wish me well," he said.

"Do well!" Chera called and blushed as she waved the scarf after him.

He turned his horse about and galloped off.

"Where's he going?" she asked.

"I guess he's going to fight for you," I explained, not remembering my medieval protocol too well. Chera held the blue scarf in both hands, close to her heart, and looked out over the battlefield with concern.

"Hey, hand me that napkin." David pointed a greasy finger at Chera's scarf.

The Blue Knight Picks My Daughter

Chera drew it even closer. "It's not a napkin. It belongs to the prince."

"Whatever." And he just used the back of his hand. So did Zach.

Some of the competition was entertaining, like when the knights, trotting by on their horses, dropped giant rings over pegs. The Yellow Knight was terrible at this and was disqualified right away. But when the Blue Knight hit all his targets, the whole blue section cheered and roared, especially Chera. Sometimes the Blue Knight would look over at Chera, and she would wave the scarf. He would nod and keep sweating and keep riding.

For the next competition the riders had to chop an apple in two with a sword. The apple was on a post, and the knight had to run past on his horse and whack the apple when he got close enough. If he did this right, the two halves of the fruit would fly off in opposite directions and applesauce would splatter the knight's face. The Red Knight was terrible at this and whacked the pole, bouncing back so hard he fell off his horse. (The blue section may have been the most unsportsmanlike. Of course, David and Zach lead the thumbs-down cheer, which didn't help much.)

The Blue Knight looked over at Chera again, wiped the applesauce from his face with the back of his hand (just like my husband!), and prepared for the next event: the joust.

When Zach saw the two knights pick up their long spears, he started to cheer. (This is what he had been hoping for ever since they had carried those silly scarves out with them earlier.)

I was a nervous wreck. One second I was watching the battle; the next second I was watching Chera. The joust.

Chera. The joust. Chera. She was holding the scarf close to her face (pinky out) and biting her lip. I glanced over at David and Zach and saw them waving their turkey bones and leading the chant, "Blue! Blue! Blue!" And where was that dessert cart? Surely at $23.50 per person they would roll out a dessert cart.

Each knight kicked his horse into a gallop, and all the cheering seemed to cease as the crowd took a collective breath and held it. The horses kicked up fresh sawdust and some new odors. As the knights drew together, they lowered the long lances until they were pointed at each other's chest. By now Zach had figured out just how a jousting match worked, and he dropped the turkey bone and put his greasy fingers over his eyes.

The knights clashed at full speed. The lances bent like fishing poles and one of them snapped in two.

The Blue Knight fell off backward and landed in the sawdust (and other soft things on the floor). The blue section gasped, and the yellow section cheered but quickly hushed when they saw the Blue Knight pull himself to his feet, cast away his helmet, and draw his sword.

As the Yellow Knight passed by, he tossed away his lance, slid off his horse, and drew his own sword. Chera pulled the scarf up to her face and peeked over the edge. The Blue Knight was walking with a limp, he was breathing hard, and his hair kept getting into his eyes. Things weren't looking good for the Blue Knight.

With lots of bad acting, the knights raised their swords and lashed out at each other. The heavy metal clanked only inches from their faces and sparks flew every time metal hit metal. Zach had picked his turkey bone back up and was now

The Blue Knight Picks My Daughter

stabbing at the air like a brave knight himself, his face glowing with grease. David had dropped his turkey bone and had covered his eyes and was now peeking through his fingers at the battle.

The swordplay waged on much longer than our appetizers had lasted. The Blue Knight, bad leg and all, would jump and bend and drop and roll and sometimes duck just before the blade would have beheaded him—I'm sure. Chera was squealing and yelling, "Go, Blue!"

Just as Blue tripped and fell backward and Yellow raised his sword to lunge at the downed knight, Blue shot his sword forward and buried it deep into Yellow's armpit. Yellow had the strangest look on his face, like Zachary sometimes gets when he sits down at the supper table and realizes I've already put a helping of green beans on his plate. The Yellow Knight staggered about, keeping the Blue Knight's sword clasped beneath his armpit. He looked at the yellow section as if to say, "Sorry, guys." David and Zachary already had begun the cheer, "Blue! Blue! Blue!"

I looked over at Chera, and she was clapping. I thought she might have been tearing up a bit, but that could have just been the excitement.

Now the Blue Knight called for his horse. He rode in a circle, waving and accepting the cheers (even people from the red and green sections were cheering for Blue now). When the cheering began to slow, and Chera sat back down—probably thinking he had forgotten about her—the Blue Knight steered his ride to the wall in front of us, climbed from his saddle and over the railing. Chera stood up, coming to about his belt buckle, and gave him his scarf back. The knight took the scarf and waved it about. Up went another roar.

Then he extended his hand to Chera, and Chera (without even looking back at me or her father!), placed her hand in his and followed as he led her through the crowd and toward the front, where the king sat, watching the whole night of games.

"Where's Chera going?" Zach asked, not wanting to be left out of any fun.

"Keep an eye on him," David said into my ear. "I'll grab Yellow Knight's sword and challenge him if I have to."

"Shhh," I said. "Watch what happens."

My tiny daughter was led to a giant chair right next to the king and was seated there. Soon someone handed her a bouquet of roses and draped a robe over her shoulders, and then, from behind her, someone lowered a sparkling crown onto her head.

Chera gripped the roses tightly, just as she had the scarf earlier. She held her head regally as the king announced, "Ladies and gentlemen, please acknowledge your love and honor for the princess of the castle!" Ever so slightly, Chera turned her head from one side (to the green and yellow sections), and they roared, and then to the other (the red and blue sections), and we roared. David was clapping and Zach was clapping and turkey grease was flying everywhere.

The Blue Knight led Chera back to us and thanked us for playing along. Chera still had her flowers and the Princess banner they had draped across her shoulder. We hugged her and told her she was a beautiful princess. Zach wanted to know if it was fun sitting up in the little box with the king and was she ever scared of falling out.

As we left the restaurant, people—strangers—bowed to Chera and said things like, "Long live the princess." Chera played along and grinned and returned the bows.

The Blue Knight Picks My Daughter

It had all been a big game. The Blue Knight was supposed to win from the very beginning. He was supposed to fall off his horse and limp around and appear defeated, just like we were supposed to eat an entire meal without a single piece of silverware.

Even though all that had been orchestrated, I couldn't help but think about the way Chera had been rescued, how she had held her head high, the way she had walked with shoulders back and flowers held close to her heart, the warm way she had smiled (even at her little brother!). For a brief moment, Chera saw herself as the king saw her. She saw herself in his eyeballs—beautiful and royal.

All I had seen was that the battles on the sawdust floor were just a big game. Not Chera. A knight in shiny armor had rescued her. She had been adopted into royalty, and she had accepted her new role as a child of the king with grace and honor.

I really would have cried right about then, but I didn't have a napkin, and I had turkey grease on my fingers.

Face to Face

See what I mean? God is at work in our daily lives even when we think things might be falling apart, even when we think things are in chaos all around us. One of the stories from the Old Testament (one that never got a whole lot of Flannel-Graph attention when I was growing up) is the story of how Moses wore a veil over his face after he had met with God and then stood before the people. He knew that God's glory, reflected in his face, was fading, and that the people would notice. When that happened, Moses feared the people would become discouraged. But—and here's the best part—in *The Message* Paul explains that:

Whenever, though, they turn to face God as Moses did, God removes the veil and there they are—face to face! They suddenly recognize that God is a living, personal presence, not a piece of chiseled stone. And when God is personally present, a living Spirit, that old, constricting legislation is recognized as obsolete. We're free of it! All of us! Nothing between us and God, our faces shining with the brightness of his face. And so we are transfigured much like the Messiah, our lives gradually becoming brighter and more beautiful as God enters our lives and we become like him.

—2 Corinthians 3:16–18

So I believe that everything that might at first appear to be aimless stumbling about—like driving cross-country in a minivan, like trying to figure out how we're going to buy diapers next week, and like trying to figure out what Momma was doing with a paring knife in the bottom of her purse—can really be seen as "an opportunity in disguise," an opportunity to see God at work, to see him pulling back the veil to show us his face so that ultimately "our faces [may be] shining with the brightness of his face."

To see your reflection in his eyes, that's what I hope for you, because if that happens, I know three things are true about you: you're very, very close to God; you're facing in the right direction; and *you have your eyes open!*

So keep those peepers glued on God; you'll be amazed at what you'll discover.

CHONDA PIERCE INFORMATION

For other Products (videos, CDs, cassettes, etc.) by Chonda
   Pierce, call 1-800-953-7878 or visit www.chonda.org.

For Adult Preacher's Kids International information contact:

   Second Row, Inc.
   P.O. Box 9066
   Murfreesboro, TN 37133-9066
   Phone: 615-848-5000
   Fax: 615-848-0407
   E-Mail: The2ndRow@aol.com
   Website: www.chonda.org

For concert availabilities and management:

   Michael Smith & Associates
   2605 Link Drive
   Franklin, TN 37064
   Phone: 615-794-5763
   Fax: 615-591-5694
   Email: michaelsmithmanagement@email.msn.com

Chonda Pierce on Her Soapbox

Chonda Pierce

In a lather about life's little details? Lighten up with Chonda Pierce!

Pet peeves been trailing mud all over your nice bright outlook? Let Chonda Pierce help you clean up your attitude with a little deep-cleansing, sparkling-fresh humor! Chonda's wacky stories won't just get you laughing so hard you'll forget what was bugging you; they'll go deeper, illustrating profound spiritual truths.

As a Christian, it's easy to assume that life's little sticking points aren't something you should bother God with. It can be hard to go to him with the "petty" details of your day, because they seem exactly that — petty. But God wants you to share all of your life with him.

So when your day and your temper both seem like a wet bar of soap — hard to get a grip on — don't work up a lather! Pick up *Chonda Pierce on Her Soapbox* instead. You'll get more than a chuckle — you'll discover that God is deeply interested in everything about you.

Softcover 0-310-22579-5
Audio Pages 0-310-22978-2

Pick up a copy today at your favorite bookstore!

It's Always Darkest
Before the Fun Comes Up

Chonda Pierce

Life might not be no joke right now — but laughter is on the way!

There are two kinds of laughter. One is a hollow hilarity that masks pain too deep for words. The other is a full, joyous laugh that sounds triumphantly on the far side of life's dark passages.

"Chonda serves up stories of heartfelt feelings and of God's most uplifting gift—the grin after the grim."
—Barbara Johnson

Comedian Chonda Pierce knows about both kinds. In *It's Always Darkest Before the Fun Comes Up*, this spunky preacher's daughter will do more than tickle your ribs. She'll touch the place in you where laughter and tears dwell side by side. She'll show you the deep wisdom of a merry heart. And with humor and honesty, she'll reveal the God who knows how to turn life's worst punches into its more glorious punchlines in his perfect time.

Softcover 0-310-22567-1
Audio Pages 0-310-22553-1

Pick up a copy today at your favorite bookstore!

Tales from the Ark

*Written by David Pierce
and Chonda Pierce
Illustrated by Matt LeBarre*

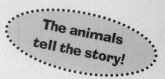

The animals tell the story!

The story of Noah will never be quite the same after these tales are told! Experience this favorite Bible story from a different perspective — the animals'. In *Tales from the Ark*, the animals share their stories for the first time ever. As you follow their adventures, you'll meet a very strong Skunk, a Ferret who gets lost, Turtle Doves who have a dark, scary secret, and other interesting characters.

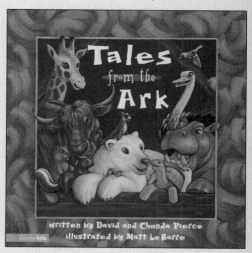

In this account, humorist Chonda Pierce and her writer-husband, David, have created a collection of funny and memorable stories that kids ages 4-8 (and their parents!) will love. *Tales from the Ark* weaves together inspiring Bible stories that share the story of Noah while it introduces and reinforces Bible truths.

Hardcover 0-310-23218-X

Pick up a copy today at your favorite bookstore!

Four Eyed Blonde
Video and Audio

On the heels of her remarkably successful videos *Having a Girls' Night Out* and *On Her Soapbox*, Chonda Pierce is back and funnier than ever with *Four Eyed Blonde* video and audio. Never at a loss for words, Chonda has shared her unique sense of humor with over a million people. In the course of an hour, she has the audience laughing, crying, and closer to understanding God's grace in the midst of trial.

Available on cassette, CD, and VHS.